Life *from a* KINGDOM PERSPECTIVE

Viewing the world as God sees it

Gregg Madden

PRIMIX
PUBLISHING
THE WRITE CHOICE

Primix Publishing
East Brunswick Office Evolution
1 Tower Center Boulevard, Ste 1510
East Brunswick, NJ 08816
www.primixpublishing.com
Phone: 1-800-538-5788

Published by Primix Publishing: 10/23/2024

ISBN: 979-8-89194-296-7(sc)
ISBN: 979-8-89194-374-2(hc)
ISBN: 979-8-89194-297-4(e)

Library of Congress Control Number: 2024916419

Contents

Preface

Words spoken by God, Jesus, and the Holy Spirit are *italicized in red* for identification purposes. Pre-written poems and writings are highlighted in blue for identification purposes. Also, the names of some associations, persons, places, and other details have been changed to respect privacy.

As the author, I do feel that context, or the circumstances surrounding a passage of scripture, is integral to its true meaning. However, for readability purposes, I cannot explore every possibility for the interpretation of every passage. To help ensure accuracy, I have studied the context of the passages used in this book in detail. As the reader, I would encourage you to explore the before and after verses of scripture used, especially if there is any doubt about the meaning.

Lastly, please understand that every individual is created uniquely, and because of that, each personal relationship with God will have similarities and differences. Please keep an open mind while reading and realize that not everything in the spiritual realm is black-and-white. Some ideas and situations will relate strongly to certain individuals and not so much to others.

This book is intended to help you, the reader, grow closer to God and to put powerful biblical truth to work in your everyday life. My goal as the author is to get out of God's way and allow Him to work, reaching as many individuals as possible with His truth.

Introduction

For I know the thoughts that I think toward you, says the Lord. Thoughts of peace and not of evil, to give you a future and a hope. (Jeremiah 29:11)

I chose this scripture to introduce this book for a reason, so we can remind ourselves that God is on our side, He is for us and not against us. His focus is toward the peaceful, prosperous future He has planned for us. That's what God is focused on, but what are we focused on? Even in talking with born again believers, I still hear things like this: "So, if He is for me, then why are things so difficult?"

In counseling with people over the years I have found many who focus on their troubles and the troubles around them, as if they are in this life all alone. If you know Jesus Christ as your Lord and Savior this is absolutely not true. As born-again believers in this day and time, we have every opportunity to experience a close personal relationship with our heavenly Father through Jesus Christ. *Life from a Kingdom Perspective,* is about the ability to see things as God sees them and not as the world sees them. The Bible is our guide. God's Word lays out the principles that we are to follow and shows us how we are designed to operate as His children. But it's not always easy to get to that place where we trust and rely on Him, always, even above our own understanding. This can be tricky because most of us, even if we were brought up in church, were taught and encouraged to rely on ourselves. That's the way of the world, not of God, so naturally we would have trouble getting away from the basics we have been taught our whole lives. But that's the key, "naturally," looking at things in the natural is worldly perspective, but looking at things spiritually, as God sees them, is Kingdom Perspective. One goal for this book is getting to that place where we can see things as God sees them. In doing that we will look at common challenges and frequently asked questions based on my experiences as an ordained minister, a business owner, husband, son, father, and a child of God.

Hello, my name is Gregg Madden and my intended purpose for this book is to relay biblical truth, as well as life experiences related to a daily walk with God. For me, life did a turnaround when I truly placed my faith and trust in Him. It was a difference as clear as black-and-white, or light and darkness. My failures, perpetual bad decisions, and despair were left far behind, and I eventually grew into success, wisdom, guidance, and hope for the future. I firmly believe that this book did not come to you by accident or happenstance. *Life from a Kingdom Perspective* was written for you, wherever you are in your walk with God, and for the non-believer who was curious enough to pick up this book. The goal is to help establish or grow your personal relationship with God through Jesus Christ and the Holy Spirit. It's only because of this relationship that we can redirect our focus and truly begin to see and live *Life from a Kingdom Perspective*.

Let's get started!

ONE

Kingdom Perspective vs. Worldly Perspective

Let's look at Jesus's words:

"I have manifest Your name to the men whom you have given me out of the world. They were Yours, You gave them to Me, and they have kept your word" (John 17:6).

In this verse Jesus makes it clear that as men and women, we can belong to Him as we walk through this life. Yes, Jesus was speaking about His disciples, but in verse 20 of the same chapter He ties us in as well. He says: *"I do not pray for these alone but also for those who will believe in Me* *through their word;"* (John 17:20). In this verse, "those" refers to us, you and I and all who know Jesus as our personal savior. In John chapter 17, Jesus prays not for us to be taken out of this world, but that God would keep us *"from the evil one"* (John 17:15) right here in the midst of this world. Jesus makes it clear that we, as believers, belong to Him and not to this world. Understanding this truth helps us stay away from the temptations of this earthly life and set ourselves apart from the world to serve Christ in all we do.

> *"They are not of the world, just as I am not of this world. Sanctify them by Your truth, Your word is truth"* (John 17:16–17).

The word "sanctify" in this verse means to set apart or declare holy. In describing the ones He is praying for in verse 6, Jesus says *"they have kept your word."* This is imperative to living life from a Kingdom Perspective. The ground floor, the beginning, is knowing God and knowing the Word. The challenge is living according to His word and not according to the world. Keeping God's commands according to the Bible, when sin is all around us, separates us from the world. And those of the world will notice the difference.

To begin to see the difference between a Kingdom Perspective and a worldly perspective, let's look at some specific situations. First, let's look at the area of finance. Many people, including myself, have experienced lack or struggled in this area at some point in life. Let's set up a typical hypothetical situation when it comes to struggling with money. Even with two incomes a certain couple has gotten themselves into debt, to a point where they cannot afford basic needs. A house payment, two car payments, credit card bills, a personal loan, and pretty soon they can't meet the monthly demand they have placed on themselves. Somethings got to give, if they make all these monthly payments, they can't afford food and gas, if they buy food, gas, and basic necessities they can't pay all of their bills. If they don't pay at least the monthly minimum, creditors begin to tack on late fees and the situation goes from bad to worse.

The first way to attempt to deal with this is from a worldly perspective, using earthly wisdom, which is how the couple probably got here to begin with. Here's how James, brother of Jesus, describes worldly wisdom:

> *Who is wise and understanding among you?*
> *Let him show by good conduct that his works*
> *are done in the meekness of wisdom. But if*
> *you have bitter envy and self-seeking in your*
> *heart, do not boast and lie against the truth.*
> *This wisdom does not descend from above, but*
> *is earthly, sensual, demonic. For where envy*
> *and self-seeking exist, confusion and every*
> *evil thing are there.* (James 3:13–16)

Conventional earthly wisdom says you need more money to get out of this situation. "Hmmm, how do we get more money? "Oh, I know, part time jobs" the couple says. Now the husband and wife are both working sixty to seventy hours a week. They have very little time together, and when they do, they're too exhausted to enjoy it. But at least their financial situation is getting better, right? Wrong, there may be more money coming in, but the situation has brought more expense into the mix. More fuel and vehicle maintenance, more miles mean more tires and brakes, plus the vehicles themselves wear out faster. More expense for lunches, clothes, and necessary items for the second job(s). Now, as James said, the self-seeking aspect of trying to fix the problem in their own strength has brought envy, strife, confusion, and every evil thing into their lives. Envy eventually causes each spouse to think the other has it better than they do. Here's some very typical thoughts that could arise during this situation.

"I'm working my tail off to get us out of this situation she created, yet she's got a nicer car than I do! Since we are making more money now, it's high time for me to get a new vehicle."

OR

"He has more time off than I do, yet all he does is sleep, leaving me to do all the housework. I know, I'll start doing only my own laundry and clean up only after myself."

I could go on with more examples, but you get the idea. Now the couple is placing blame on each other, they have brought in more expense and are often angry toward one another when they do have any time together. Now they are working against each other instead of being as one flesh. Stress and strife have brought division, and any unity is now gone. And, they have serious marital problems that could lead to one or both spouses looking for attention elsewhere. This will be easy to find, since both are spending more time with coworkers than they are with each other; what's next?

We will leave our hypothetical couple right there for a while. We can easily see the truth in this example, using worldly wisdom brings problem after problem instead of solutions. But let's take the same desperate situation and see what God's Word says.

First, I want to dispel any wrong thinking right now before we go any further, because I don't want to give anyone the wrong impression. This is *not* a name it claim it, blab and grab it, or stake it and take it kind of book, and I am not that kind of author. What I am is a spirit filled child of God who believes God's promises to us are real and His word is genuine. I believe 2 Timothy chapter 3 which says, *"All scripture is given by inspiration of God, and is profitable for doctrine, for reproof, for correction, for instruction in righteousness, that the man of God may be complete, thoroughly equipped for every good work"* (2 Tim. 3:16–17).

If we truly believe the Bible is the inspired word of God, then why would we not believe the promises it contains? No, God is not a genie who grants wishes, nor is the Bible a book of magic spells that can be repeated to bring results. The Bible contains godly wisdom that can be manifest in our lives by faith, for the purpose of doing His work. With that said let's look at our couple's situation from a Kingdom Perspective using godly wisdom.

This couple is struggling to make ends meet, so what does the Bible say about our provision, money, and finances?

Look what Jesus says in Matthew chapter 6:

> *No one can serve two masters, for either he will hate the one and love the other, or else he will be loyal to the one and despise the other. You cannot serve God and mammon. Therefore I say to you, Do not worry about*

your life, what you will eat or what you will drink; Nor about your body, what you will put on, is not life more than food and the body more than clothing? Look at the birds of the air, for they neither sow nor reap nor gather into barns; Yet your heavenly father feeds them. Are you not of more value than they? Which of you by worrying can add 1 cubit to his stature? So why do you worry about clothing? Consider the lilies of the field, how they grow; they neither toil nor spin; And yet I say to you that even Solomon in all his glory was not arrayed like one of these. Now if God so clothes the grass of the field, which today is, and tomorrow is thrown into the oven, will he not much more clothe you, oh you of little faith? Therefore do not worry, saying, "what shall we eat?" Or "what shall we drink?" Or "what shall we wear?" For after all these things the gentiles seek. For your heavenly father knows that you need all of these things. But Seek first the Kingdom of God and His righteousness, and all these things shall be added to you. Therefore do not worry about tomorrow, for tomorrow will worry about its own things. Sufficient for the day is its own trouble (Matthew 6:24–34).

Let's take another look at the same hypothetical couple, this time they have the same mountain of debt, but they face it differently. This time they come together, each confessing their part in the frivolous spending that led them to where they are now. Instead of blame, they come together admitting their faults and working together to see where each one can cut back and do with less. As one says, "I can start taking my food from home and cut back on eating out for lunch"; the other says "hmm, ok, if you do that, I will quit going to the coffee house twice a day." They pray together asking God what else He would have them do about this situation. Yes, they created this debt, God did not, they will have to work out of it, but God is there to help lead, guide, and direct when they call on Him. Let's look closer at our scripture:

"Seek first the kingdom of God and his righteousness, and all these things shall be added to you. Therefore do not worry about

tomorrow, for tomorrow will worry about its own things" (Matthew 6:33–34).

Now the couple has come together willing to work on this problem, praying together, asking for guidance, and trusting God. This is seeking first the Kingdom; this is using godly wisdom to defeat the enemy. We have read what James, brother of Jesus, says about earthly, sensual, demonic wisdom, now let's look at what the book of James says about godly wisdom:

> *"But the wisdom that is from above is first pure, then peaceable, gentle, willing to yield, full of mercy and good fruits, without partiality and without hypocrisy. Now the fruit of righteousness is sown in peace by those who make peace"* (James 3:17–18).

It's easy to see the difference between earthly wisdom and godly wisdom according to scripture. The first, earthly wisdom, brings envy, strife, confusion, and evil. But godly wisdom brings peace, mercy, gentleness, and guidance. Now, let's look back at our couple. By working together, reading scripture together, and praying together, they have brought unity into the marriage instead of division. Since each admitted their faults in the situation, humility is now at work rather than pride. Because they were both willing to yield, they have each helped create peace instead of placing blame… what's next?

To answer what's next in each situation we need only use common sense. Using earthly wisdom the situation is headed for disaster if it continues its current path. However, using godly wisdom brings peace into the marriage and we see a real chance of it working out, hope has replaced despair. Here's the way God's word sees it, as recorded by Solomon, son of David in the Book of Ecclesiastes:

> *Two are better than one, because they have a good reward for their labor. For if they fall, one will lift up his companion. But woe to him who is alone when he falls, for he has no one to help him up. Again, if two lie down together, they will keep warm; But how can one be warm alone? Though one may be overpowered by another, two can withstand*

him. And a threefold cord is not quickly broken (Ecclesiastes 4:9–12).

With two working together and God in front, there's a whole new outlook, a Kingdom Perspective has been born. My wife and I have been living life from a Kingdom Perspective going on sixteen years at the time of this writing. But it wasn't always so, we have fully experienced life from a worldly perspective; desperation, fear, stress, worry and hopelessness come to mind from those days. A little later, chapter 4 will show God's work, grace, and mercy taking place in our lives and how He led us to our personal transformation. How we were able to put off the old man and put on the new man, with God's help and *only* by His grace! Chapter 2 will show just a glance of the darkness we lived in before God became first place in our lives.

But before we move into the next chapter, I want to introduce a sense of urgency that becomes more and more real to me as time passes by. Whatever you have been putting off when it comes to God, it's time to get on with it—going to church, starting a Bible study, taking care of ongoing sin in your life, or maybe even writing a book—as you navigate these pages, explore the possibilities of working godly wisdom and a Kingdom Perspective into your own life. I want you to remember that none of us are guaranteed tomorrow, so let this book help you get serious about whatever it is you need to do. Here are some thoughts on how short life is. Facebook is one of the social media platforms I have found helpful for ministry, especially during Covid in 2020. I wrote this poem for my family on Christmas Eve 2022, and later posted it to The Teaching Room Facebook page:

Time Flies

We have all heard the phrase, and we know that it's true,

Your little one is born, now she's taller than you!

Where did the time go? How did it happen so fast?

We must hold to the things, that we know will last.

The older we get, the faster time goes,

Why does this happen? Does anyone know?

A ten year old kid, waits for a year to pass,

Christmas or his birthday, finally gets
here at last.

The child then grows up, time keeps going by,

Now he's fifty years old, seems like the blink
of an eye.

A tenth of our life, is a pretty big piece,

But a fiftieth of life, goes much faster indeed.

So now as adults, we have the same year,

But the time seems much shorter, till the next
one gets here.

Now as we move on, down the path of our life,

It's so very short, no time for worry or strife.

So cherish each day, make the best of your time,

Try to leave something good, for those
left behind.

This life is a blessing, and we all have a gift,

So let's use our potential, to give others a lift.

As this poem comes to end, I leave with
this thought,

The best things in life, they can never be bought.

So thank you for reading, as I leave you
with love,

And let's keep our purpose, in the one up above!

God Bless, Yours in Christ,

—Brother Gregg

TWO

My Story

Revelation 12:11 tells us,

> *"They overcame him by the blood of the lamb and by the word of their testimony. And they did not love their lives unto the death."*

Most times it's hard to see how far the Lord has brought a person unless you know a little about where they have been. Testimony is a powerful thing; it encourages others and shows God's abundance in many cases. Nothing I say in this book is designed to glorify the enemy, but rather, overcome him and bring hope to some who may be, or have been in similar situations.

Like many people, I had caring, loving parents who raised us in church. I gave my life to God at a young age, and for a short season I lived like it. However, before long I began looking more toward the world than toward God. As a teenager, I began the typical drug and alcohol lifestyle as a lot of kids did growing up in the late seventies and early eighties. But unlike most people, for me, this lifestyle helped create addictions that would become daily habits well into my adult years. Pretty soon I left all thoughts of God and church far behind, beginning a long season of selfish living, which led me into some very dark places over the years. For me, rock bottom came much later in life, brought on by selfish living, drugs, alcohol, and a total disregard for others. At this point, I was living for me, trying to make things happen in my strength, with little if any regard for God. This is the direct opposite of living life from a Kingdom Perspective, this is life from a worldly perspective.

Perspective is the way we view things based on our own current situation and our past life experiences. A person's perspective can give a whole different meaning to any word or phrase, as I have witnessed so many times. One such occasion was this:

I call on about forty different small businesses for work. I was in one of these facilities when I saw a very familiar face coming toward me at a distance. "Hey, Jerry," I said, "long time no see!" As our paths brought us closer together, I could see his whole countenance change. It appeared to be a look of anger mixed with confusion coming upon his face. In a loud voice, he shouted, "What did you say?" Right then I realized that the words, "Long time no see," were probably not the best choice of words to say to a blind man! I had used that phrase many times and never had that result, but because of his unique situation, my friend interpreted the words very differently than most people would.

In the same way, a close relationship with God changes the way we view things, and the way we react and respond in a given situation. A Kingdom Perspective, or seeing things as God sees them, is a fruit of a close relationship with Him. Therefore, the closer we get, and the closer we stay to our heavenly Father, the more our nature and character reflect Christ in all we do.

Until you have spent some time in darkness, you can't appreciate the light. Let's look at how

Jesus put it in Luke 7, talking about a woman who anointed His feet:

"Therefore I say to you, her sins, which are many, are forgiven, for she loved much. But to whom little is forgiven, the same loves little" (Luke 7:47).

For me, by the time I began to walk with God at almost forty years old, I had accumulated a great deal that I needed forgiveness for, as I confessed, repented, and changed my ways.

Yes, I said accumulated, a sinful lifestyle doesn't usually come out of nowhere, but grows deeper and darker over time, at least mine did. Paul writes about this process as he describes how the gentiles (non jews representing the unsaved) live apart from God in Ephesians 4,

This I say, therefore, and testify in the Lord, that you should no longer walk as the rest of the gentiles walk, in the futility of their mind, having their understanding darkened, being alienated from the life of God, because of the ignorance that is in them, because of the blindness of their heart; who, being past feeling, have given themselves over to lewdness, to work all uncleanness with greediness (Ephesians 4:17–19).

That was me. Toward the end of my life without God, I was in the dark, past feeling. I had given myself over to all kinds of lewdness, uncleanness, and greediness, trying to fill a great void inside of me. But it didn't start out that way. Let's back up and look closer at the path that led away from God, the path I chose early in life that led to darkened understanding and being alienated from a life with God for a season.

As a teenager and a young man I had hope and confidence as I set out into the world. But the ignorance, or lack of knowledge that was in me, along with worldly wisdom, led me to think I didn't need help, that I could do it all on my own.

Early on, around the age of twelve, I was introduced to marijuana by a young man whose family moved to our small town from the city, we'll call him Clayton. At first Clayton and I didn't get along at all, in fact, we actually got into a fistfight the first day we met! Soon after that, Clayton and I began to spend a lot of our time together after school and during summer breaks. We were usually at one another's houses or running rampant in the countryside, fishing, hunting, or just hanging out. For a short time we were almost inseparable, then, a couple of weeks into our sophomore year of high school, we became at odds with one another, seemingly out of nowhere came friction between us. That led to us not seeing each other for about a week or so, longer than ever in our short three-year relationship. One Saturday night my mother came and found me, saying, one of Clayton's parents is on the phone, have you seen him? I explained that we had an argument and I had not seen him outside of school in about a week. The next day I was awakened with terrible news, my friend had taken his own life. This was a tragedy that rocked our small town, but even so I didn't realize the effect it had on me until years later.

I continued smoking pot, experimenting with other drugs, tobacco, and alcohol which grew into daily habits before the end of high school. I remember a friend who came and stayed in our neighborhood every summer saying something that should have really caught my attention, but it didn't. She said, "I've been here for a week and every time I've seen you, you've had a beer or a joint in your hand, or both." It didn't alarm me at all, in fact, in my youthful ignorance, I thought this was "cool." But I was becoming more and more angry about everything, walking slowly away from God, producing fruits that were anything but godly. Soon, I developed a reputation for being crazy, which in our world meant out of control, and that's exactly what I was. I would often fight for no good reason, doing whatever I wanted, when I wanted, with no regard for others. I drank, used drugs, frequented bars, and was just plain reckless, bringing problem after problem on myself. At the time, I just thought I had really bad luck, I was deceived, but God's Word tells us exactly what was going on:

> *"Do not be deceived, God is not mocked; for whatever a man sows, that he will also reap. For he who sows to the flesh will of the flesh reap corruption, but he who sows to the spirit will of the spirit reap everlasting life"* (Gal. 6:7–8).

Looking back, it's easy to see I was bringing corruption and failure into my life by the way I lived. One incident pretty much sums up my life at the time. I was young, driving an old Ford truck, a 1973 model, in excellent condition until this night. I'm definitely not condoning this behavior, but back then I drank and drove most all the time and I just threw all my empty beer cans into the back of the pickup (didn't want to litter). Today I thank God that by His grace I never hurt anyone besides myself with my selfish actions of this kind. This particular night, I had been drinking and using as I headed out for the evening on the familiar country road I traveled often. For unknown reasons I was traveling 70–80 mph when I lost control on a sharp curve and rolled the pickup. Witnesses said it rolled three times and came to a stop upright, as this happened, most of the beer cans were thrown out all over the place, and the truck came to rest with the cab crushed, the windshield shattered, and two flat tires blocking the entire road where no one could get by. When I opened my eyes, I was laying in the passenger floorboard, with my head hanging out the open passenger door looking up at the night sky. As I pulled myself out and stood up, I realized there were about ten people there, between stopped vehicles and those who had come out of their houses. As I stood up, I remember seeing the faces all in disbelief as I began walking away from the vehicle unharmed. The people began telling me I needed to get out of there before law enforcement showed up, one man went to his house and called a tow truck (no cell phones back then). Another neighbor got a trash bag and began cleaning out the few remaining cans and other incriminating evidence in and immediately around my truck. I'm still not sure why all those strangers wanted to help me stay out of trouble, pity, I guess. When the wrecker driver arrived, I still remember his exact words as we were standing there. He looked around at the surrounding ditches and over the fences into the fields at all the empty cans reflecting the light from a flashlight beam. He said, "I only have one question for you; where's the beer truck you hit?"

But there was no beer truck, just me, all alone, going way too fast and out of control. This statement described my entire life at the time. To make matters worse, I actually repaired the two front tires and ended up having to drive the wrecked truck for almost a year out of desperation. Imagine the truck, cab smashed to the point that the passenger side door would not close, so it had to be wired shut with a coat hanger. The windshield entirely shattered to the point that the driver's side upper corner would fall inward, so I had to keep the sun visor down in order to hold the windshield up. I lost my job and my apartment because I went to jail a few times for overnight stays and missed work until my boss could no longer tolerate it, so I quit before I was fired. My desperation, anger, and hopelessness became worse, I pushed those who loved me away and even became homeless for about two weeks. I used every drug available to excess, including but not limited to, alcohol, marijuana, meth, cocaine, LSD (paper acid), and whatever else came my way. My pent-up anger caused major problems with all my relationships and even with strangers.

One night, after spending hours at the bar, I ended up in jail not knowing how I got there. The next morning, as I awoke in a jail cell, after falling off of the top bunk and hitting the concrete floor, I began to contemplate my surroundings. The first thing I saw was a large man under a thin blanket on the bottom bunk in my cell. As I looked out through the bars, the first thing I heard, was people banging on the bars to the tune of a heavy metal song as they chanted: "Six, six, six, the number of the beast, hell and fire, were born to be released." Once again, I chose to ignore the obvious message here and began chanting along with the song, which I knew very well. I had no idea why I was in jail, only remembering the beginning of the evening before, as I had walked into a bar around 7:00 p.m. and paid my "open bar" fee, which allowed me to drink as much as I wanted until 10:00 p.m. (Yes, they actually did that back then.) A little later everyone who had been picked up the night before was put into the "drunk tank" as we awaited the Judge for sentencing. The room was a larger version of a jail cell, with a single open toilet, a sliding window with a view into a small office, and a telephone in the center. As the room filled it became crowded, and people began to talk about how they got there. When I was asked that question, I said "I honestly don't remember, I don't know where my truck is, and I was brought in with no keys, wallet or I.D., same as I told my good friend whom I called to come bail me out." As I said that, two guys in the drunk tank spoke up, saying, "we know how you got here," they had been at the same bar. They told of how when the bar closed at 2:00 a.m., we all walked into the parking lot, and I climbed into my wrecked Ford pickup. As they told it, I drove out of the parking lot toward a police officer directing traffic in the street, when I apparently zoned out on his waving flashlight and headed right toward him. He had to move out of the way to keep from being hit, and I kept driving until I was out of their sight. I thought, *Man I've done it now!* I thought about friends and family who had told me for years that I was going to end up dead or in prison if I didn't change; I guess I finally proved them right, I thought in despair. After what seemed an eternity, the judge walked into the small office, slid the window open, and began calling names. Each person would maneuver through the crowd as they were called up and read their charges. Of course my thoughts ran wild as I cringed with every name called and I thought, What will I be charged with, assault, DUI, DWI, attempted murder, all of it? How long will I be in prison? Then I heard my name and worked my way to the window. Time stopped as I could hear nothing except the judge's voice as he spoke. He said "Mr. Madden, you are charged with public intoxication, how do you plead?" I said "Guilty, your honor," and I waited to hear the rest of the charges, the bad ones. The next words out of his mouth shocked me, "$90 and time served," he said. I remember standing there, as it sank in, and I began shaking uncontrollably and had to be moved out of the way. I'm not sure why I was temporarily incapacitated like I was in that moment.

Soon after, my name was called again and the guard said, "You made bail" and I was led to an office where I was handed my two belongings, shoelaces and a belt. They would give me no information beyond that, where was my truck? Who bailed me out? Where were my keys? My wallet? But all I really wanted was to get out of that building, so I grabbed my shoelaces and my belt and walked out the door. I saw my friend, Steve, standing in the parking lot, laughing like crazy at my appearance. Long sleeve white dress shirt, wrinkled, torn, unbuttoned and untucked.

My middle of the back length, rock star looking hair going every which direction, my pockets hanging out of my pants with shoelaces and belt in hand. Steve answered my questions as he handed me my keys and my wallet with several hundred dollars in it, only missing the amount he had paid to bail me out. He drove me to my wrecked truck, which was parked in a fast-food restaurant parking lot, blocking the exit. By this time it was midday and cars were exiting the drive-thru having to do a U-turn because my truck was in the way. My friend found my truck right there, both doors standing wide open, keys in the ignition, wallet in the seat. He closed the driver's door, wired the passenger side shut, and came to bail me out. At the time I thought, *Man, I got lucky!* So I got in my wrecked truck and drove off to continue defiling myself.

As bad as I was, I still had a few friends and family trying to help me, aside from those I had driven away. My dad always said "When you go to jail, don't call me," so I never did. My sister Diane scraped up her money and gave it to Steve so he could come bail me out one time. I started to separate myself from those who still cared about me, maybe out of shame, or guilt, or wanting to protect them from me. Even in my messed-up state of mind I still tried to respect those who cared about me by staying away during my dark times.

I could tell more than a dozen other stories about my life of darkness during those years: times I really shouldn't have made it, times there was literally a gun held on me (more than once); one incident where a knife was held to my throat, and several times where I was on the other end of the knife or gun; times I woke up after an obvious brawl, with crusted blood on my face, bruises, body aches and a pounding head, not remembering where I had been; other vehicle wrecks, many physical fights (some ending with bodily injury), stories where I committed breaking and entering and other serious felonies. But instead I will move on from this darkness for now because you have heard enough to know what type of lifestyle God has delivered me from, and that was the main intention of this chapter. I chose to give detail about one of my jail stays and the truck wreck because looking back we can easily see God's hand in those situations. I cannot explain how I didn't end up dead or in prison on a number of different occasions. All I can say is God can work things out, even when we don't acknowledge Him in our lives. It's amazing how much more He can do when we get to that place where we seek and acknowledge Him on a regular basis.

Finally, with help, when I was twenty years old I got a steady job and a newer, undamaged truck, still angry at the world, but barely doing enough to hold this job down. I worked with a good group of guys and my boss saw good in me, even as I showed up late on occasion, hung over, and still living in darkness. I learned to do enough to get by. I became a good employee, stayed out of jail, and kept up the outward appearance of a responsible young man. From 7:30 a.m. to 5:30 p.m. Monday through Friday I did pretty good, at least outwardly, although behind the scenes it was a different story. I was still running wild outside of work, certainly not living up to my full potential, using drugs, drinking, and pursuing all ungodly worldly pleasures. All actions have consequences, either good or bad, and soon one of the women I had been with became pregnant. At twenty-two years old, despite how I got here, I had to decide what kind of man I wanted to be. Would I dodge my responsibility as I had most of my life? My girlfriend made it easy for me to escape, as she was about 10 years older than I was, and told me she was having the baby, but was not expecting anything from me—the perfect opportunity for me to escape back into the careless, selfish, lifestyle I had always known.

THREE

A Chance for Change

The Bible tells us in 1 John 1:

"If we say that we have no sin, we deceive ourselves, and the truth is not in us. If we confess our sins, He is faithful and just to forgive us our sins, and to cleanse us from all unrighteousness" (1 John 1:8–9).

So, at some point along the way, the question becomes, is the truth in me? Am I really a sinner in need of repentance, or is that just a bunch of self-righteous hogwash those Jesus folks like to say? Yes, at this point in my twenty-two-year-old life, I had given myself over to the world and came to realize it. Even though I had given my life to the Lord and was baptized years earlier, I saw myself on the "other side" of things. Now, with a pregnant girlfriend and no clue what to do, I don't ever remember consciously asking God for guidance or direction about my next steps. Instead, I heard bucket loads of advice from co-workers, friends, and other worldly sources. It was all pretty much the same thing: "Why buy the cow when you're already getting the milk for free?" People mostly told me how I was young and didn't need to be tied down this early in life. I was getting advice from a worldly perspective. "Don't get married, just live together and see if it works before you commit." Or "Just pay a little child support and see your kid on the weekends."

I got more comments and suggestions than I could listen to, most thought I wasn't mature enough to handle the responsibility, and they were right! But something deep down inside of me could not stand the thought of a child running around, not knowing who their father is, because of me.

Nor could I just be a part-time father, sending cards on birthdays and at Christmas, barely being part of my child's life. Wait a minute, these were good thoughts, good advice, no person had told me these things, so where were they coming from? Remember earlier when I said, "*something* deep down inside of me?" Well, that was my worldly perspective at the time talking. Looking back on the situation from a Kingdom Perspective, I now know that the prompting inside of me was a *someone*, not a something.

So, I made a decision based on my conscience, whom I now know as the Holy Spirit within me. For once I felt like I wanted to do the right thing, the responsible thing, instead of taking the easy way out. So, I got married to my first wife and we had a child together, our daughter was the biggest blessing I had ever experienced in more ways than I can count. As I held my precious baby girl for the first time, she truly changed me for the better. It was like I had willingly stepped up several notches on the responsibility scale, and it felt good. Nicole was now depending on me for sustenance, for life lessons, and for guidance and direction. But it didn't feel like a burden, instead a life changing blessing had come into my dark world. I remember early on, anytime she would cry or become irritable I would lay down flat on my back with her on my chest as she almost immediately quit fussing and drifted off to sleep. I loved her so much and still do, she needed her daddy and I truly wanted to be there for her in every way.

You would think that would have been enough to cause me to give up my vices for good, but it wasn't. During my new wife's pregnancy, she quit anything that would have harmed the baby. So, naturally I went underground with my drug use, so she wouldn't be tempted. (Funny how we can try and justify our sin and make ourselves feel better.) Now I was lying and sneaking around, hiding my drug use and still openly drinking daily. Sin always has the potential to lead us into more sin, taking us deeper and darker than we ever intended. I remember times when I would leave a note early on weekend mornings, telling my pregnant wife that I was going to the home improvement store, or some other place. In actuality, I would drive to a parking lot or out by the lake and do a couple of big lines of meth, maybe smoke a joint, and then return home to my wife. Sometimes I would actually do it in the Home Depot parking lot, so I didn't feel like as much of a liar, this way, I actually *had* gone to the home improvement store.

As I said earlier, when my daughter was born it changed me in a lot of ways, but my demons were still there. I began using drugs openly again as my wife was no longer pregnant and my daughter was an infant. When she was just beginning to walk, an incident happened that changed the way I did things once again. My friend Steve had come over to my house and we were sitting around my glass coffee table as I was chopping out a line for us. He pointed to the end of the table and said, "you have an audience!" I looked over and saw my daughter holding herself up at the end of the table. Her big beautiful brown eyes, full of life, were watching me, taking everything in as I was tapping that razor blade on the glass, preparing to do drugs with my friend. That hurt me bad, but apparently not bad enough for me to give it up altogether. I went back underground, lying, hiding my faults, and deceiving everyone around me.

Aside from drug use, the first few years my wife and I had an almost storybook life raising our child. I had become a functioning addict. Things were good for a short season, my daughter was my first concern in life, she was the apple of my eye.

I tried to be the best father to her that I could be, but here was the problem, God was not first in our lives. I was trying to do it in my own strength. We went to several different churches during those years, I even gave up drugs for a short season and got baptized for a second time. I wanted to publicly confess my faith and make a genuine change, but I never developed a relationship with God, so I never put Him first place in my life. When trouble came, I went right back to trying to fix it on my own and failed. My wife and I began to have problems, and things became stressful, and it seemed there was always some kind of drama in my life. Again, in my own strength, I tried to protect my daughter from the stress and strain of our failing marriage. Somewhere along the way, I resigned to the fact that our marriage was not going to make it. At the same time, I felt strongly that I could not take the chance of my wife getting custody of our child if I ended the marriage.

I will only give limited details of the situations because my ex-wife has passed, and I don't want to expose my daughter to anything she doesn't already know that would hurt her. With that said, my first wife had developed issues that we desperately needed help with, to no avail. She became angry, depressed, and suicidal at times, several times.

Finally, at one point, my wife's problems and actions no longer just affected me, they were beginning to affect my daughter and it scared me. I knew, because of my wife's behavior, I had a really good chance of getting custody of Nicole. So I filed for divorce when she was ten years old, ending an eleven-year marriage and gaining custody of my daughter. But the battle wasn't over by a longshot, my ex-wife fought for custody. For six years, she made false accusations against me to child protective services (CPS). All of the accusations were dismissed, because they weren't true, but thirteen court dates and $40,000 later, the damage was done. For a couple of years, Nicole could only see her mother with a CPS supervisor in the room with them, which was never my intent. Those were the years my daughter would look me in the eye and tell me "I hate you Dad!" I knew it wasn't her true feelings, but it still hurt. My dad always told me I would pay for my raising, is this what he meant? When my daughter was seventeen, she moved out.

It was tough for a while, but Nicole and I have a good relationship today, and I am well pleased with the person she has become. However, when she moved out, it was about the same time my relationship with my live-in girlfriend of four years ended. Stephanie and I had lived together during this custody battle induced turmoil, with her daughter and my daughter. We were to the point of drinking three to four half gallons of hard liquor a week; plus the beer I drank daily. I had given up drugs a couple of years earlier due to the custody battle, and later, I forced myself to quit drinking, while expecting my girlfriend to do the same. Obviously, the relationship couldn't handle that, and we split up, going our separate ways. We were both messed up, mentally, physically, and emotionally. This was the beginning of my lowest point in life, but to give you, the reader hope, God is coming soon! Hang in there! It seems when my girlfriend and I split up I started going back to my old ways, all of them, *"As a dog returns to his own vomit, so a fool repeats his folly"* (Prov. 26:11).

The first thing I did after the breakup was sleep with several of my ex's friends. I'm not sure why,

I guess I thought it would make me feel better, but it didn't. So unfortunately, after that I moved on to women in my neighborhood, married or not, it didn't matter at this point. All the while drinking and using more and more as I went, it's almost like I had developed an unquenchable thirst for sin and didn't care that what I was doing was wrong.

> *"Now the Spirit expressly says that in latter times some will depart from the faith, giving heed to deceiving spirits and doctrines of demons, speaking lies in hypocrisy, having their own conscience seared with a hot iron"* (1 Tim. 1:4).

My conscience had become seared over to the point that it no longer bothered me to do wrong. I would listen to no one. I remember one of the women, or girl actually, (she was twenty-eight, I was almost forty) coming by my shop as I was working. Charlie, one of my co-workers came over after the girl left, he said, "She was wearing a wedding ring; is she married?" I said yes, he just shook his head and walked off, saying: "That's

just wrong!" I told him to mind his own *******
business, and to be glad it wasn't *his* wife! And
then I went back to work. I had officially become
the worst person I had ever been, and I didn't care.

It's no wonder I had destroyed almost every
relationship in my life, even the women I was
messing around with started to despise me. I was
now sleeping with multiple women, lying, and
making promises I had no intention of keeping.
How did this happen? I had become a womanizer,
and a liar, two of the very things I had despised
earlier in my life.

One of these women, a neighbor, actually
began to stalk me over the way I treated her. I
had come home with a woman on the back of
my motorcycle one night about two o'clock in the
morning. We will call her "Pat," she was an older
woman from across town. We had been drinking,
we walked in my house, smoked a joint, and began
doing what we came there for. All of a sudden,
around 2:30 in the morning, my landline began
to ring. I ignored it, it would stop, and then start
ringing again. Finally, I answered it, thinking it
might be a family emergency or something at that
time of morning. It was "Carla," a neighbor from

down the street whom I had also been with several times. She began screaming into the phone, "Who is that *****," she said. Apparently, Carla had been watching my house, waiting for me to come home. I hung up on Carla and immediately told Pat to get dressed and I took her home.

In my filth and lewdness, between different women, I had created a volatile and dangerous situation, not to mention the possibility of husbands finding out. I was in the darkest place of my life, and I wanted out of the very situation I had created! I checked into truck driving school, because I wanted away from these women, away from all the turmoil I had created, but I began walking with God before I could follow up with school.

To this day, even though it was over seventeen years ago, even though I have confessed, repented, and been forgiven by my heavenly Father, despite the fact that I have truly forgiven myself, and the fact that I did my best to make amends to all those I hurt through my selfish behavior, I still feel remorse when I give testimony about those days. I only discuss these actions in this book so others may see the dangers of ongoing sin, repent, and turn from it before they get to the point I had gotten to in my lewdness and depravity.

This filth had gone on for about a year, getting deeper and darker as time went by, just like Paul wrote in Ephesians 4 earlier. I had a void in my life, and I did not know how to fill it. My understanding was darkened. I was alienated from the life of God because I no longer listened to the voice inside of me. But God has more than one way to reach people when He needs to. As well as that still small voice within us, He can use other people, visions, circumstances, and many other methods, too many to list. He used a burning bush to reach Moses, and a donkey to reach Baalam. God doesn't give up easy. For me, it was one phone call that would set in motion a chain of events that would change my life forever!

FOUR

The Restoration

Therefore, if anyone is in Christ, he is a new creation; old things have passed away; behold, all things have become new (2 Corinthians 5:17).

It was sometime around spring/summer of 2006 when my phone rang, it was Shirley, my ex-girlfriend's mother. Stephanie and I had been broken up for about a year, so the phone call startled me at first, and then I became very curious. Shirley lived out of state, so she called me, because Steph and I lived in the same town. Shirley went on to say that her daughter was in a bind and about to lose all of her personal possessions. I remember saying, "What do you want me to do about it? We have been separated for a year;

I can't help her." But Shirley didn't give up, she kept on, almost begging me to help her daughter, so I finally gave in to her request. I agreed to help Steph gather her personal belongings, pictures, mementos, and basic necessities and store them for her.

As I said earlier, it was the phone call that helped change the direction I was headed, for good this time. As I began helping my ex, I realized that she had changed, drastically, and for the good. She seemed happy, content, and peaceful, so much different than she was during our four years of living together. She told me about the people who had helped her get to this place of peace and contentment by giving her life to the Lord. She then asked if I would take her to church on Sunday, since she didn't have a ride. I remember thinking how people like her, people with addiction problems, needed church, so I agreed to take her. (Strange how I didn't see myself as having any issues, even though I was still living a self-destructive lifestyle.) I had seriously damaged most of my relationships with friends and family, my mother, my father, co-workers, and my daughter, just to name a few. But change was coming soon.

Now all things are of God, who has reconciled us to Himself through Jesus Christ, and has given us the ministry of reconciliation, that is, that God was in Christ reconciling the world to Himself, not imputing their trespasses to them, and has committed to us the word of reconciliation (2 Corinthians 5:18–19).

I wasn't sure about this Jesus thing, but the more Steph and I were around each other, the more I wanted what she had. About six weeks in, I committed myself to walk with God. Through a Christ-based recovery program, I learned that I could actually have a personal relationship with my heavenly Father. This changed Steph and I for the long run, and all the people around us began to see the difference.

Some were skeptical at first, but the more we grew together in our new life, the more people saw the truth, the change was real. God was now real to us, and I knew we'd been brought back together for a reason, to serve Him. I may fill in some of the blanks later, but for now I will tell you that Stephanie and I were married in 2007 and God continued to do amazing things. A little less than a year after reestablishing my walk with God, we put Him first, even before each other, and things began to change quickly.

Not only did Stephanie and I become reconciled to each other through our reconciliation with God, but we were able to grow together and become closer than we had ever been before. I found this to be true with most of my relationships at the time, walking with God changed my relationships with others. Yes, with most I had to apologize and ask forgiveness, but that was no problem for me as humility came along with my new walk. I was also able to re-establish communication with some I had pushed away to avoid exposing them to my toxic lifestyle. Coming out of the darkness and into the light changed our world and allowed us to connect with other people like never before.

Specifically, my dad comes to mind first. We had many years of conflict during my youth and young adulthood. Later in life he saw Steph and I struggle in our relationship and with addictions before God reconciled us to himself. Dad was a very good example of the Father's unconditional love for us. Yes, he got frustrated, angry, and we even went seasons without seeing each other; but he never quit loving me. My dad knew the power of God in a person's life could bring lasting change, so he was one of the first to accept the change in us as real. In fact, he was so proud of us, he gave us his older truck as a wedding present. Dad and I are still close today, and now, as he is older, I am able to help him in his struggles.

My mom and I were also able to become close again, as we were when I was a child, something we had not had in a long time, but precious to me. And yes, I was able to be there and be that person she could count on once again during her challenges late in life. We remained close until her death in 2019.

My daughter and I were at odds as well, the divorce and six-year child custody battle had taken its toll on our relationship. She had moved out to live with a friend at the age of seventeen. She went from telling me she hated me, to coming back around to see us as we grew in Christ. In fact, at one point she gave me a copy of an essay she had written while in college, it was entitled, "My Dad, My Hero." It was not until a couple of years later that I realized the significance of the date on that paper. It was dated September 26, 2007, exactly one year after my salvation date, the day I fully committed to walk with God. I came to realize that, in less than a year, God was able to restore multiple relationships that it had taken me many years to destroy. My daughter and I are still close to this day, at thirty-four years old she still calls "Dad" when she has a problem, and sometimes just to talk or have me pray for a given situation.

I was also able to begin building closer relationships with my sister, my three nieces, and others. Some family I could not be a godly influence for when they were young, because I did not know God for myself. But every day brings new opportunity to serve Him and be that man of God that I wasn't before. In fact, I have been able to perform several family funerals and my middle niece's wedding ceremony back in 2021. This is priceless to me, for if I reach the whole world for Christ, but can't be a godly example to my family members, it wouldn't be as satisfying.

My purpose for sharing this testimony of restored relationships is to bring hope, hope to some who may be struggling in this area. No relationship is beyond repair as long as God is in the picture, if He can fix my issues, He can fix yours as well. As with all of the godly principles I discuss in this book, the ultimate purpose is for you, the reader, to put them to work in your life.

All these restored relationships are only because of my relationship with my heavenly Father, they speak to His glory and not my own. Living for God and no longer living for myself changed my character as I grew in Christ. With God's love flowing through me to others it changes things with everyone in our lives. Let's continue in Ephesians 4, after Paul talks about the process that leads to darkness, he addresses born again believers:

> *But you have not so learned Christ, if indeed you have heard Him and have been taught by Him, as the truth is in Jesus: that you put off, concerning your former conduct, the old man which grows corrupt according to the deceitful lusts, and be renewed in the spirit of your mind, and that you put on the new man which was created according to God, in true righteousness and holiness* (Ephesians 4:20–24).

So how did I go from living in darkness to living in true righteousness and holiness? In God's strength, that's how. For me, when I realized the depth of God's mercy and grace, it caused me to want to serve Christ, and help others find the freedom I had found. The bondage of sin, which had held me captive for so many years, was now broken.

We are individuals, and as such, God deals with each one of us personally. For me It seems God had delivered me from drug and alcohol cravings almost immediately, I had no desire to drink or use as I began growing in Him. To this day, I have not drank alcohol or used illegal drugs since September 26, 2006. And furthermore, I still don't miss it.

Right here some are saying "Wait a minute, I struggled for years to overcome my addiction, and still do. Why was it so easy for you?" First, let me say, it isn't easy. Serving in God's kingdom can be very challenging, causing us to trust in, and rely on Him. And, we are dealt with as individuals, while I know God delivered me from those two addictions, I had to work through plenty of other issues along the way, and I still do, things like anger, forgiveness, lust, greed, pride, shame, trust, and other issues that have the ability to harm my relationship with God. Who knows except God, but maybe the addiction factor would have been too much for me to handle? Maybe this is Him, making a way of escape so I can bear it.

I should also make it clear that Stephanie and I had lots of help during the early years of our walk. I cannot mention them all by name, but each person who was part of our personal growth early on in our walk will always be precious to us. To God's glory, we were surrounded by mentors and brothers and sisters who helped us along the way. In the beginning, Mike and Sandee Macmahon, pastors of our small church home at the time, helped us grow through that most crucial "New Christian" stage in our walk with God. Season after season, change after change, God placed people in our path for strength, support, and fellowship. Again, everyone's walk is different, but for us, we have grown through multiple stages of ministry while serving Him. Even today we are part of a solid church family where we serve, worship, and belong, which is imperative to maintaining our walk. Generations church of Granbury is now our church home.

> *And let us consider one another in order to stir up love and good works, not forsaking the assembling of ourselves together, as is the manner of some, but exhorting one another, and so much the more as you see the Day approaching* (Hebrews 10:24-25).

To God's glory, there has been one constant saving grace along the way, our service to Him. This is where I do not want to be misunderstood, our service to God is not what saved us, or brought us salvation, nor is it a burden. Salvation is a gift of God which must be received by faith. *"For by grace you have been saved through faith, and that not of yourselves; it is the gift of God, not of works, lest anyone should boast"* (Ephesians 2:8

The ability to do God's work is a blessing and an honor, and for me, service is what keeps me close to Him. After all I had done earlier in life, the fact that He forgave me, and still trusts in me to do His work, humbles me and brings me great joy. I have been given the gift of teaching, in His strength, that is the underlying foundation of my walk in serving Him.

Early on in our walk, the Lord began to mold me into a worker for His kingdom. I have showed a little of the darkness God brought my wife and I out of, now to His glory only, moving into the next chapters, I will explain a little of what He has led me into over the years since 2006. With God as the head of our lives, Steph and I began to do things we never did, or could not have done before, without God. As a fitting close to this chapter, I will use a post I wrote back in August of 2020. This was written for The Teaching Room Facebook page, which is still ongoing and just one of many ministry platforms the Lord uses to bless us. Why would I use a pre-written page to close this chapter? Because it is a very condensed version of our testimony that will lead into God's goodness and mercy, as we detail His blessings heading into the next few chapters.

This is the first mention in this book, of listening to the correct voice as we overcome the negative words that are sometimes spoken over us. You guessed it, a worldly perspective hears all the noise and negativity, while a Kingdom Perspective focuses on His promises. Here is what I wrote on that subject in August of 2020:

It Won't Last

About 15 years ago my life did a complete turnaround, no more living as the world lives. Illegal drugs, alcohol, self-indulgence, and selfish motives all gone. I began serving God.

People said "It won't last"… IT DID! I Was ordained as a minister in 2012. Next, People said, "Your relationship with your girlfriend will not work, too much water under the bridge."… IT DID WORK! Now she's my wife. In 2008-09, some said, "Your business will not make it through this recession."… IT DID MAKE IT! It's been our main source of income for well over 10 years now. Six out of seven doctors told me, "That tumor in your leg is Cancer."… IT WAS NOT! When my wife shattered her ankle People said, " It will never be the same again"… IT IS 100% HEALED!

I could go on, but by now you get the point. God is ABLE to overcome no matter what people say! Remember as Christians we are in this world but not of this world. Oftentimes, when you try to accomplish or believe for something good, someone or something will come against you. Don't let negativity win. Put your trust in God and know that He has the last word.

"Now to Him who is able to do exceedingly abundantly above all that we ask or think, according to the power that works in us" (Eph. 3:20).

No matter what you're going through, "GOD IS BIGGER!"

FIVE

Knowing Him

When I finally began to realize that only a close relationship with God could bring me the peace, joy, and contentment I was looking for, things changed drastically and quickly. Communication with God became key to my spiritual growth. Without that, I would have been headed right back into the darkness I had recently come out of. However, those around me, who had known me, were not as quick to accept that change as "real," until some time had passed. As I changed and grew in ministry, people noticed, some questioned, some accepted.

In order to hear His voice, and see Him at work, we must be extremely careful who, and what, we listen to and acknowledge. That is challenging in the beginning for most people, and there are many reasons for this challenge. First is the negativity surrounding us in this sin filled world, by non-believers, and yes, even sometimes among Christians. Those who have never experienced hearing His voice for themselves are naturally skeptical of those who have. Skepticism is nothing more than doubt or unbelief expressed. For example, early on in my Christian walk, with two coworkers, I mentioned a pastor friend of mine who felt led by God to start a church. Immediately, they both began to laugh and mock my statement, saying things like this: "Oh yeah, I'm so sure God spoke to him!" Then the other said, "If he really hears from God, tell him to give me a call with tomorrow's lottery numbers!"

Cynical talk like that can damage our faith and our ability to receive from God if we let it. It surprised me to hear that come out of their mouths, especially since they both went to church all of their lives. That's when I learned there is a huge difference between going to church and having a relationship with God! Going to church only requires a ride to get there, communicating with God requires faith. So, when I ran into this type of skepticism, who did I choose to listen to? Someone who mocked me, laughed at me, and tried to make me look ignorant, or the one who never left me during my darkest times, and forgave my transgressions? Easy decision, at least for me it was.

At that time I had to make a choice, I chose to believe God's Word over and above all else. But even Jesus experienced negativity from others, it harmed His ability to do ministry around those unbelieving people. Look at what Matthew's gospel says:

> *Now it came to pass, when Jesus had finished these parables, that He departed from there. When He had come to His own country, He taught them in their synagogue, so that they were astonished, and said, "Where did this Man get this wisdom and these mighty works? Is this not the carpenter's son? Is not His mother called Mary? And His brothers James, Joses, Simon, and Judas? And His sisters, are they not all with us? Where then did this Man get all these things?" So they were offended at Him. But Jesus said to them, "A prophet is not*

without honor except in his own country and in his own house." **Now He did not do many mighty works there because of their unbelief** (Matt. 13:53-58).

This passage shows us some powerful things to consider. Jesus is our example, and we will face the same things He did. First, the people we are closest to, those who know us best, are the ones who can affect us the most. They are often our biggest challenges when doing God's work.

Next, look at the two things that seem to cause Jesus trouble in His ministry, offense and unbelief. Mark's account of the same event, tells it a little differently, let's look: *"Now He could do no mighty work there, except that He laid His hands on a few sick people and healed them. And He marveled because of their unbelief. Then He went about the villages in a circuit, teaching"* (Mark 6:5–6).

The fact that Jesus *"marveled at their unbelief"* shows us that even Jesus was surprised by their response. He should have been. If we get to where we believe the people we are about to talk to are going to reject us, then we are the ones demonstrating doubt and unbelief. Look at the words in

Mark 6:5, *"Now He could do no mighty work there."* If other people's unbelief could cause Jesus's work to suffer, what can it do to us? Be careful what and who you listen to, as I already said, but more importantly, look at His example of how to deal with this. Verse 6 says that after Jesus marveled at their unbelief, He went about teaching, right back to doing God's work. That's what we should do as well, get right back in the flow of serving the Father! Jesus walked according to what He taught His disciples, and what He still teaches us through His word today. When Jesus sent out the twelve apostles to do ministry on their own, He told them this:

"And whoever will not receive you nor hear your words, when you depart from that house or city, shake off the dust from your feet" (Matt. 10:14).

Just as Jesus moved on after experiencing the unbelief in His hometown, He tells his followers to do the same. In telling them to *"shake off the dust from your feet,"* Jesus is symbolically saying, don't let their unbelief remain with you. Shake the dust from your feet and move on to the next house, or town, or ministry project. Time is short, seeds are planted, and the Lord has more for you. Don't get bogged down by someone else's unbelief, or lack of enthusiasm toward your ministry. Chances are, God already has that next person in place to encourage you as you move forward.

Now let's look at what Jesus did *not* do; He did not respond as some Christians today would have. He did not take offense and tell all His friends how He was disrespected. He did not try to get as many as possible to side with Him, causing a church split. He did not feel sorry for Himself for the way He was doubted, complaining to the pastor and eventually leaving the church.

Each time we doubt, murmur, or complain, we are wasting time that we could be using to serve God. Jesus didn't doubt, murmur, or complain, neither should we. We have to know when it's time to move on, that comes from knowing Him and being able to hear His voice.

Christians understand that Jesus came to earth, suffered and died, was resurrected, and went to sit at the right hand of the Father. Most even know this was done so our sins could be forgiven. He paid the price of our disobedience for us, so we can spend eternity with Him. Some even know, that eternity starts now, right now, in *this* life, we can fellowship with God, with His spirit dwelling in us. But it's not always easy to see the things that may be causing division between us and Him in our daily walk.

Being forgiven our trespasses and admitting our sin, requires humility, plain and simple. Until we admit, confess, and turn from our sin, we will not be able to truly receive forgiveness. This is not just a one-time thing; we must keep a check on ourselves as we walk with Him. Sin has a way of creeping in on us, slowly, deceptively, doing damage as it quietly pulls us away from God. It did with me.

Earlier, I told you that my girlfriend and I had separated, then I came to the Lord as a result of seeing her changed life? It was during this time that we were growing closer to God and each other, when sin attempted to move back into our lives, quietly and discretely. We had been back together about eight or nine months, serving God as best we could. I was beginning to accept my role as a teacher and was leading a small group in our recovery program. Then it happened, Stephanie was about to lose her temporary place to stay, she had to move out and had no place to go. So I said, move back in with me, after all, we were doing great now, getting along with each other, growing together in God. We were even talking about getting married, so she moved back in. It was only a few days later when I got a wakeup call from God, both literally, and figuratively. Look what scripture says about it:

"If I had not come and spoken to them, they would have no sin, but now they have no excuse for their sin" (John 15:22).

Once we have accepted Jesus as our Lord and Savior there is no longer an excuse for sin, no way to even attempt to justify it without consequences. What we need to do at this point is humble ourselves, confess, and repent. Get our pride out of the way and give the situation to Jesus. This done with genuine sincerity will get us back into His grace, back into doing His work. Jesus told us, *"If we confess our sins, He is faithful and just to forgive us our sins and to cleanse us from all unrighteousness"* (I John 1:9).

The Lord showed me how sin can damage a relationship with Him in a very clear and straightforward way. More details on how that occurred, and how God helped me take care of it in chapter seven, Hearing His Voice. But for now, we need to focus on the fact that sin creeping back into our lives while serving God will stunt our growth in Him.

The next thing we will discuss in this chapter that can harm our spiritual growth, is failure to acknowledge God and what He has done in our lives. If we truly want to hear His voice and receive godly guidance, we must acknowledge Him. As Jesus tells us:

"Therefore whoever confesses Me before men, him I will also confess before My Father who is in heaven. But whoever denies Me before men, him I will also deny before My Father who is in heaven" (Matt. 10:32–33).

As part of the natural, normal growth process, children go from being completely dependent on their parents to being independent and able to make it on their own. Somewhere along the way, usually around the early teenage years, they begin to display signs of their need for independence. Being ashamed or embarrassed of their relationship with their parent(s) is a common phase as they grow to adulthood. Eventually most get past this and learn that a relationship with their parents is rewarding and extremely helpful in life. It's much the same as we are born again into the kingdom of God. Look what Jesus says:

"Assuredly, I say to you, whoever does not receive the kingdom of God as a little child will by no means enter it" (Luke 18:17).

A "little child" in a new relationship with God should fully trust and rest in Him. As we grow in our spiritual life, there will be occasions when we are tempted to deny or at least downplay God's role in our lives. Just like a child in the natural world, we must get past what other people think to receive maximum joy and benefit from our relationship with our heavenly Father. That's when the power of God can work in and through us.

"Trust in the Lord with all your heart, And lean not on your own understanding; In all your ways acknowledge Him, And He shall direct your paths" (Proverbs 3:5-6).

Acknowledging God came very easy to me, maybe because my life was going nowhere good before I recommitted to walk with Him. When my life began to change for the good at forty years old, I knew exactly why and so did everyone around me, whether they would admit to it or not. I didn't have a problem acknowledging His presence in my life, it was too easy to see, I could not ignore or deny His presence. I talked with Him all day long every day, with every decision I consulted Him early on in our relationship. In fact, I got accused of being a "crazy person" at work one day for talking to God as I worked. The only thing I thought was crazy, was not sharing how good God had been to me since I started seeking Him. I wanted no part of life on my own anymore, and still don't, it doesn't work for me.

But remember, everyone is different, every relationship with God is different, what's easy for one person may be a difficult struggle for another. Through the years I have seen a number of people who were opposite me in the area of acknowledgement.

I specifically remember one man who was employed by a company I serviced as part of my business. He began to ask me questions about church and tell me about the church he was going to with his wife and kids. I started to notice, every time someone else would walk into the room, he would hesitate, or stop talking altogether. I even asked him about it, he said, "Yeah, these guys here don't really know that about me, and I would like to keep it that way." It saddened me to hear that. I ministered with him and prayed for him and moved on.

God has ways of showing Himself that leave no room for doubt when He needs to make an undeniable appearance. As I said, I have no problem giving glory to God for everything, big or small, everything I have is because of Him anyway.

One day I was working with a helper, Trish, in my service business as we began to run out of the supplies we needed to finish our route that day. As I began to pull into the parking lot of a large retail superstore, I saw that the parking lot was full all the way to the street. I knew that if we didn't get in and out of there quickly, we wouldn't have time to finish our last vending stops before the businesses closed. I began to pray for favor over the situation as I drove up and down a couple of aisles, and Trish began to laugh. She said, "Do you really think praying is going to help you get a parking place?" The second she stopped talking, a man began to back out, almost hitting us, I tapped the horn and backed up, so he could get out and I pulled in. It was the very closest available non-handicap parking spot directly in front of the door. I didn't say a word about it. I just said, "come on" and I got out and began to walk toward the store. It wasn't long before she couldn't stand the silence between us as we walked into the store. She said, "No way that was God. That man was just ready to leave, that's why he backed out." I said, "You can choose to see it that way; I see it differently." As we loaded two large shopping carts and walked toward the checkout, we noticed there were at least three to five sizeable orders waiting in every line. But, before we could even choose the line we wanted to be in, an employee grabbed the front of my basket and led us to a register she was just opening up. Almost instinctively, I looked upward and said, "Thank you Lord." This time my helper just smiled and shook her head at me, thinking I was crazy. She laughed and mocked me all the way to the truck.

It was two days later, Trish and I were getting ready to head out, we had a big route that day. As we were loading the truck, I said "Check the strap on that item, it looks a little whomperjawed to me." I'm not sure if you have heard that term, but obviously she had not. She began laughing, "what does that even mean?" I explained that it meant off kilter, askew, or not working properly. She laughed and accused me of making it up, all day long she gave me a hard time about it, jokingly of course. She would use the word to excess for the rest of the day, "look that car is whomperjawed." Or "look at that whomperjawed man walking his whomper-jawed dog." This went on all day, she had probably used the word ten or twelve times, when something incredible happened. We had driven around working for over eight hours and were finally fin-ished and headed back toward our small-town during rush hour traffic. As I pulled up to the long line at a traffic signal, I noticed something that floored me, I could not believe what I was seeing! I nudged Trish and pointed to the Cadillac Eldorado in front of us. The license plate read exactly this, in big bold personalized letters: "WMPRJD"

Trish was shocked and speechless for the longest time. It took two or three cycles to get through the red light and she just stared at that license plate the entire time. Finally, with a very confused look on her face, she said, "How did you do that?" I told her there was no way I could have ever made that happen. I thought her head was going to explode, trying to figure that out with logic, but I had to remind her of something more. At that time, there were close to 20 million registered vehicles in the state of Texas where we live. There could only be one "WMPRJD" license plate. As we got through the light and began to drive off, she asked again "How did you do that?" Again I said, I could not have orchestrated that even if I'd tried. She finally said, "I know." She was silent and just stared out the window for the remainder of the twenty-five-minute ride home, but she couldn't stand it. As I dropped her off, she was getting out of the truck when she said, "No really, how did you do that?" Even she could not claim that was coincidence.

Earlier I told you that God has ways to reach us that leave no room for doubt or argument, this was one of those ways. This changed the way she thought about things from that point forward. My wife and I both witnessed this young lady giving glory to God on more than one occasion after that. This is priceless motivation for me, watching people think the blessings of God are exaggerated, and then being a witness to their entire attitude changing. It humbles me and gets me excited at the same time.

Though I cannot explain every detail of why or how this happened, all I can say is we serve a big God. It still amazes me to think about it, our God, picked one car out of 20 million and arranged things so it would be right in front of us. Apparently, He did all this to help change the thoughts of just one girl. And it worked! So, if you don't already do this, begin to acknowledge Him in all your ways and see what happens in your life! God can do amazing things when He has a willing vessel to work with.

SIX

The Power of the Word

Now that we have discussed the damage that can come from listening to the wrong voice, let's talk about how to listen for the right voice. God is definitely not limited in the ways He can communicate with His people. Let's start by looking at His most common method of reaching believers. One of the most important ways God can reach us, as believers, is through His Word. In the King James version of the Bible, we have 66 books containing 31,102 verses of scripture available to us, for guidance, direction, confirmation, and communication. Yes, I said communication.

The Word of God is an often-overlooked method that He frequently uses to guide us through a given situation and to help us grow in our spiritual walk. When we face a situation where a decision is required, either good or bad, we can see what the Bible says about it and let that be a starting point to lead us in the right direction. For believers, the Bible should also be our bottom line, our measuring stick when communicating with our Heavenly Father. If we are seeking Him and *we think He is leading us in a certain direction, we need to use God's Word as* confirmation. If the direction we think He's leading us does not line up with scripture, or contradicts scripture, we need to pause and rethink. This helps us take some of the human emotions and inaccuracies out of play and focus on the genuine truth. It's the most solid, yet simple way to ensure we are listening to the correct voice. For people who say, "it's just a book," I would refer them to the gospel of John, chapter one.

> *In the beginning was the Word, and the Word was with God, and the Word was God. He was in the beginning with God. All things were made through Him, and without Him nothing was made that was made. In Him was life, and the life was the light of men.*

And the light shines in the darkness, and the darkness did not comprehend it (John 1:1–5).

Let's look at the last line of this passage, *"the darkness did not comprehend"* the light. In other words, in this dark, sin filled world, spiritual things do not make sense. That's why we must look beyond this world to get to the truth. The Word is a mighty weapon, available to us by faith, to help us navigate the spiritual realm. Notice how the words "He" and "Him" are capitalized in these verses as they've been throughout this book when referring to God. This is often called reverential capitalization, the practice of capitalizing words that refer to a divine being or deity. This helps us easily see the Word of God as a person, not a thing, and furthermore, the Word is a living being, hence the name, "The living Word of God." Jesus was the Word in the beginning. The Word was with God when He spoke everything living into existence, through the Word, and then, John 1:14 happened: *"And the Word became flesh and dwelt among us, and we beheld His glory, the glory as of the only begotten of the Father, full of grace and truth"* (John 1:14).

So, the Word (Jesus) was God, in the beginning, then the Word became flesh and dwelt among us here on earth. About thirty-three years later, after defeating the enemy, Mark's gospel tells us what happens next with Jesus: *"So then, after the Lord had spoken to them, He was received up into heaven, and sat down at the right hand of God. And they went out and preached everywhere, the Lord working with them and confirming the word through the accompanying signs. Amen"* (Mark 16:19)

So, is that the end of the story? Jesus at the time of creation as the Word, then He became flesh, dwelling among us, going up to the right hand of the Father, but at this point, He's not finished yet. Look at what the book of Revelation says:

Now I saw heaven opened, and behold, a white horse. And He who sat on him was called Faithful and True, and in righteousness He judges and makes war. His eyes were like a flame of fire, and on His head were many crowns. He had a name written that no one knew except Himself. He was clothed with a robe dipped in blood, and His name is called The Word of God (Revelation 19:11–13).

Jesus comes back once again, and once again, "His name is called The Word of God!" Jesus goes full circle for us, as the Word, from the beginning to eternity with Him, and every moment in between. He will never leave us or forsake us, His word is power, and He left us the Holy Spirit when He went to sit at the right hand of the Father. Jesus tells us this in John's gospel:

If you love Me, keep My commandments. And I will pray the Father, and He will give you another Helper, that He may abide with you forever— the Spirit of truth, whom the world cannot receive, because it neither sees Him nor knows Him; but you know Him, for He dwells with you and will be in you. I will not leave you orphans; I will come to you (John 14:15-18).

Jesus is here to guide and direct us through everything we face, good or bad. The Word is available to us 24/7 to help us in carrying out our kingdom responsibilities. The Helper, or the Holy Spirit, was sent by Jesus, from the Father, to dwell within us and guide us into all truth, including but not limited to the Word of God.

Doubt and unbelief can prevent us from ever having a close relationship with God and even damage an existing relationship. But that's not all we have to be aware of, there are two other common areas that can keep us from growing close to Him, sometimes, most times, it begins without us even realizing it. Ongoing sin, and failure to acknowledge God publicly in our lives, can both cause us to not grow as close to Him as He would like us to be. Let's look deeper at both situations. Let me use a popular scripture as an example:

> *"Therefore submit to God. Resist the devil and he will flee from you. Draw near to God and He will draw near to you"* (James 4:7–8).

Most Christians will recognize this passage of scripture, some even know that it's out of James chapter 4, but fewer realize that verse 8, as I have written it above, is intentionally incomplete. This is the way we often hear these two verses quoted in the church. This is what we want to hear about our relationship with God. When we draw near to Him, He draws near to us. That's comforting, but what we don't want to hear is the conditional part of this verse. Now, let's look at James 4:7–8 in its entirety:

> *"Therefore submit to God. Resist the devil and he shall flee from you. Draw near to God and He will draw near to you. Cleanse your hands, you sinners; and purify your hearts, you double-minded"* (James 4:7–8).

I have heard that verse quoted incompletely, as often, or maybe more often than I have heard it in its entirety. We don't want to think about that part of it, the part where we can't sin, or do whatever we desire. A big part of us being close to God in this life is the fact that we must choose to live a holy life, to the best of our ability at least. We must understand that God's grace is definitely not an excuse to sin. However, we don't have to be perfect, God knows we are imperfect, that's why He sent Jesus to die for our sins. He took the punishment for our sins, past, present, and future, to secure our ability to have a relationship with Him—to fellowship—with our Father. But there is more to it, let's continue reading in James chapter 4, the next two verses tell us more about what it takes to live life close to God:

> *"Lament and mourn and weep! Let your laughter be turned to mourning and your joy to gloom. Humble yourselves in the sight of the Lord, and He will lift you up"* (James 4:9–10).

This is James, brother of Jesus, telling us that humility is required if we want to draw near to God and have Him draw near to us. Why is humility and living a clean life so important to our relationship with God? Because, until we recognize and acknowledge our need for His wisdom, guidance, and direction, we are not ready or able to hear from Him. And, sometimes, we just don't listen. Let's look at this from a human, worldly perspective and see if we can gain a better understanding of the situation.

I have seen this same scenario multiple times, with many different people and with diverse circumstances. I have in fact, been guilty of it myself more than once. In one particular case, as I was working as an associate pastor in a certain church we were part of, when a woman in leadership approached me. She was looking for advice in a situation she was dealing with, so she began to describe the details. As I was listening, the Holy Spirit began to reveal wisdom and guidance to me, real advice that pertained to her exact situation. She paused for a second, but before I could speak, she began talking again. I waited as she described the same situation in different words, repeating that she wasn't sure what to do about it. As I started to respond, she began talking over me again. This happened at least two more times in that conversation, finally she said, "Thank you" and walked away. *What?* I thought to myself as I watched her walk away.

Humility causes us to seek advice, underlying pride, busyness, or even short attention span can cause us to miss the wisdom we were seeking to begin with. It's important to have fellowship with God on a regular basis as part of a healthy relationship with Him. It's also important that fellowship with our Father includes us listening, as much or more than praying and asking. I have had many people, when facing a hard choice or situation, tell me this: "I have prayed, and I just can't tell what He wants me to do; I'm not getting an answer."

I usually ask, "When was the last time you clearly heard His voice?" The answer is often, "Oh, I don't know, I think when I was dealing with such and such problem." Well, that may be part of the issue, only going to God when you have a problem. If you asked me right now, "When was the last time you heard His voice?" My answer would be, "About twenty minutes ago when I told Him good morning and He said good morning back", then I listened further and felt peace about working on this book for a while and going to work a little later on this morning. He speaks to us in our spirit most often. You can seek guidance, yes, but right now focus on the fellowship. There was no major problem, just talking and listening. Some readers are already becoming skeptical of these statements. However, the more you have daily communication with your Father, the easier it becomes to hear and trust Him in a big decision situation. Just like any relationship, it takes work to be successful, think about that. If you never said, "good morning" to your spouse, never asked,

"How was your day today?" or never had casual conversation, how would you ever come together when a big problem or decision came up? You wouldn't, because you wouldn't really know each other, and it's the same in our relationship with God. If you only go to Him when you have a major problem, it's really hard to hear Him, because you don't truly know Him. I'm getting a little ahead of myself, preparing for chapter 7, Hearing His Voice, but first a couple words of advice.

The more people you tell about your personal relationship with God, the more doubt and unbelief you can experience, and we have already discussed some of the problems that can cause. Your personal relationship with God is just that, it's personal. It should not be secret, but certain aspects of our relationship with our heavenly Father are best kept private. Yes, it's ok to share how God works in your life, in fact, you should, but treat it like all relationships in your life, be careful what you share, or it can cause problems. Just as you wouldn't share the most intimate details of your marital relationship with just anyone, in the same manner we must be careful to protect our closeness with God in our relationship with Him.

Earlier, I said the Lord wanted me to go to work a little later in the morning so I could work on this book. Please remember, I own my business and I work for myself, by myself, most days. Back when I was a mechanic working for someone else, I would never have gone in late and gave my boss the reason I told you about. "Hey boss, I felt led by the spirit to come in late today because I'm working on writing a book." I can hear Him now, gravelly voice, cigarette hanging out of his mouth, "Well, I hope God and the book your writing can support you, because if this happens again you won't have a job!"

The closer you stay to God, the more you will be able to discern what to say and what not to say to each individual person you encounter. For example, my pastor, Alan Latta, and I share things about ministry that we wouldn't tell some people, but because we know each other, we know it's safe to discuss hard things. This comes from knowing God and knowing each other and allows us to carry out God's work together. This type of trust—being able to share godly experiences with one another in confidence—is priceless. It helps us both grow and experience more than we ever could on our own. I have been blessed to have had many mentors, friends, and associates in ministry over the years, whom I could trust without fear of ridicule or mocking. As mature Christians in the body, we often need each other's help to maximize our ministry efforts and yes, even to build up our own personal relationship with God as we grow. Often times, when we counsel, mentor, teach, or preach to others on a given subject, we grow stronger in that same area. Paul says in First Corinthians 6, *"But he who is joined to the Lord is one spirit with Him"* (1 Cor. 6:17). As we grow close to our heavenly Father in spirit, we should also be growing closer to our brothers and sisters in Christ. That's how God's family is designed to work.

One more thing before we move on, when using God's Word for guidance and direction, interpretation becomes extremely important. Let's use a scripture we have already discussed as an example. *"In Him was life, and the life was the light of men. And the light shines in the darkness, and the darkness did not comprehend it."* (John 1:4-5)

In translating that verse correctly, we can see that the lost, or people with a worldly perspective, cannot understand the spiritual things of God. So, how do we make sure our interpretation is accurate from a Kingdom Perspective? Yes, hearing His voice, yes, guidance from the Holy Spirit, but first we need to make sure that our interpretation of a verse lines up with the Word. In this case it's pretty easy to find confirmation, *"For the message of the cross is foolishness to those who are perishing, but to us who are being saved it is the power of God"* (1 Cor. 1:18).

You see, this verse confirms John 1:5 and goes a step farther. Not only can the lost, or those in darkness not comprehend, but they see it as foolishness, because they have not received Jesus for themselves. I call this parallel scripture. Let's see if we can find confirmation from another passage that we have already discussed in this book.

> *This I say, therefore, and testify in the Lord, that you should no longer walk as the rest of the Gentiles walk, in the futility of their mind, having their understanding darkened, being alienated from the life of God, because of the ignorance that is in them, because of the blindness of their heart* (Ephesians 4:17–18).

Do you see how even one phrase, "having their understanding darkened" confirms our interpretation? Simply put, scripture backs up scripture. If you can't find confirmation in the Word, then you should reconsider your interpretation and ask God for understanding.

Also, many times, the Word will contradict an interpretation, or a word we "think" we may have heard from God. If you are about to do what you think God told you, then you find out the Bible says otherwise, confirm it in another passage as we discussed, then *stop* acting on what you think you heard. God will never lead you into sin or in a direction away from Him. The more you grow in your relationship with Him, the more clear and easy communication becomes. At some point, a conversation with God should be just as "real" as a conversation with another person. In fact, He wants you to be able to communicate with Him anywhere, anytime, that's the power of a relationship with our heavenly Father. And remember, true communication requires listening as well as speaking. More on that in the next chapter.

SEVEN

Hearing His Voice

Everything we have discussed in this book so far has led up to this chapter. Hearing from God is the only way to truly grow to a place where we live life from a Kingdom Perspective. And as we already know, hearing requires listening. God's guidance through His Word, through spiritual prompting, and through personal communication, are key to seeing things as God sees them.

Faith is key to communicating. If a person has doubt and unbelief when it comes to hearing God, then they won't hear Him. We already looked at those people in Jesus's hometown who did not believe. Scripture says He could do no mighty work there because of it, yet He moved on and we saw plenty of mighty works among people elsewhere. The only ones the doubters hurt were themselves. Skepticism is natural, that's why we must grow in the spirit and move away from some of the natural tendencies that can damage our spiritual growth.

Unbelief is contrary to genuine faith; they rival one another, and usually, one will become dominant in a given situation. Now let's discuss the opposite scenario, where faith is dominant.

Let's say God is moving at a revival meeting and there are genuine healings and miracles being experienced. As this occurs, the level of unbelief drops with each work of God until it is almost non-existent. Any skepticism has been disproved by His works and God's power is free to flow, unhindered by negativity. There may still be a few in the crowd who are skeptical, some even speaking against the happenings as if they are a hoax, but by this time faith is dominant and unbelief has no impact on the situation. Unbelief has been overcome by faith. This is why you will sometimes see meetings where the Holy Spirit is moving, and no one wants to leave. There have been gatherings scheduled for one or two days that continued on for weeks. Once the healings and miracles start, people will come back daily and bring their friends and family expecting more. I dare say that if an atheist or agnostic were to end up at one of those meetings, there is a strong chance the experience could change their beliefs. Just like unbelief can spread, dominant faith is often contagious. As the Bible says, *"Now faith is the substance of things hoped for, the evidence of things not seen"* (Heb. 11:1).

Hebrews 11 is considered "The Faith Chapter" by many Christians. It lists some of those in the Bible who are counted as having great faith. The people mentioned in Hebrews 11 are sometimes referred to as members of the "Hall of Faith." What I want us to focus on for the purposes of this chapter is why these mentioned are counted as having great faith. Great faith prevailed in each case despite the fact that they made plenty of mistakes. First let's look at Abraham according to Hebrews 11, *"By faith Abraham obeyed when he was called to go out to the place which he would receive as an inheritance. And he went out, not knowing where he was going"* (Heb. 11:8). We see from this scripture that Abraham was obedient, he trusted God by following His direction even though he did not know where he was going. But how was he able to connect to God's leading and prompting? He was "called," scripture says, it was only by hearing God's voice that Abraham was able to go out according to God's instruction. When you think about it, it takes faith to hear God's voice, and God's voice often leads us in a direction where we have to trust Him by faith. That may be a big part of the reason why Hebrews 11 says this, *"But without faith it is impossible to please Him, for he who comes to God must believe that He is, and that He is a rewarder of those who diligently seek Him"* (Heb. 11:6).

When we diligently seek God, we will find Him. When we find Him and continue to seek Him by faith, we will learn to hear Him. Why is it impossible to please God without faith? Because, before we can walk in obedience, before we can do what He wants us to do, we must first *know* what that next step is. That type of knowing is imperative in getting us to the place where we are lining up with His will for us, and it takes faith to communicate with Him. That's where the power comes from, the power to overcome challenges, the power to do things in God's strength that we could never do on our own. Hearing His voice is the beginning of being able to walk in that power.

Now that we know the importance of hearing God's voice as part of a daily relationship with Him, let's get specific. First, let me say that "hearing" God's voice most often does not require the use of our physical ears. Yes, He can definitely speak in an audible voice when He wants to, but He mostly speaks in ways that require and build our faith, as well as the faith of others around us. These ways of faith building will change as we grow in relationship with Him. When we use our faith on a regular basis, it becomes stronger over time, much like physical exercise builds muscle. Strong faith keeps us in a place where we are able to hear His voice in the moment He wants to reach us.

I promised specifics, so I will use a very recent example to start. As I was preparing to preach the Sunday morning sermon on Memorial Day at my home church, Generations Church of Granbury, the Lord spoke to me through His still small voice by the Holy Spirit who dwells within us. Sometimes my own thoughts try to enter in and complicate things as I am preparing a message.

That was the case this particular morning as I was trying to work in a scripture that did not belong with the message. I heard the Lord say three words, "keep it simple." As I continued, a few minutes later, I heard it again "keep it simple." By that time I was about to head out and start my workday, so I said, "Got it Lord," and headed out the door. As I stopped at a nearby grocery store to get supplies for my workday, I ran into a woman who had attended our Bible studies and whom we'd attended church with years ago. We talked, said our goodbyes and began to walk off in different directions when she called me back. "Are you still teaching and preaching," she asked? I answered yes, and then she said, "I'm glad, because you're really good at relating to people and getting the Word across." I said thank you and started to walk away as she stopped me again, saying, "I think your message is always good because you keep it simple!" That got my attention, about twenty minutes earlier the Lord had spoken the same thing to me as I was preparing a message, the exact same three words, "Keep it simple." He had spoken it to me twice. Now a woman I hadn't seen in two or three years, and with whom I hadn't attended church in seven or eight years, tells me the exact same three words. I call it confirmation, something the Lord wanted to make sure I heard, and acted on, for the purposes of the message I was working on at that time. Was it a surprise to me when God spoke in this situation? No, not really, I pray for guidance before, during, and after every message I prepare, before I sit down to work on this book or any ministry project, so it's no surprise but anticipated. What we have here are two common ways God uses to reach us in one example. First the still small voice within, second, words from other people.

I need to give praise to God right here for leading us to a church where the Holy Spirit is free and able to lead guide and direct His people. As I preached and gave testimony of His guidance that morning at my home church, several people spoke my friend's words before I could say them! "Keep it simple" they said from their seats. Not only did they not mock my hearing from God, but they joined in, knowing from their own experience that God was speaking to me through this woman.

On another occasion the words of a sister at a Bible class I was teaching on a Wednesday night helped me see and appreciate our home church even more. She said, "I really needed this word, and I almost didn't come tonight," and then she explained what she meant by that. Casually she mentioned that she had expressed her hesitation to her nineteen-year-old daughter, who encouraged her to come and to not ignore the prompting of the Holy Spirit. When our kids grow in their own relationship with God to a point that they encourage us, that's priceless! As the name clearly states, we have many parents at Generations Church who have raised their children in the ways of the Lord from a very young age as the Bible advised, *"Train up a child in the way he should go, and when he is old he will not depart from it"* (Prov. 22:6).

When it comes to hearing from God, these kinds of testimonies can cause skepticism among non-believers of course, and sadly, unlike those at my home church, even among some born again Christians. "Who is this guy that he thinks he hears from God?" It seems ridiculous to some who have never experienced this type of communication, and their doubt lines up exactly with scripture itself. God warns us that we will face skepticism, the apostle Paul even helps prepare us for it, *"For the message of the cross is foolishness to those who are perishing, but to us who are being saved it is the power of God"* (1 Cor. 1:18).

Jesus became flesh and dwelt among us so He could take the punishment for our sin, and we could be forgiven. Once we have confessed, repented, and been forgiven, then we can begin building our relationship with God. People who have never experienced a relationship with Him for themselves see this as foolishness, but, for me and many others, the power of God is real and accessible through a close, personal relationship with Him, because of Jesus, through the Holy Spirit. Jesus knew that we would need more than just the Bible, more than just words to read, if He expected us to do His work after He went to be at the right hand of the Father. We would need 24/7 access to God, just as Jesus had during His earthly ministry. Jesus prepared His disciples to move into the next season by communicating with God through the Holy Spirit. We are still in the same New Testament season as the early church, look at His words in John's gospel:

"I still have many things to say to you, but you cannot bear them now. However, when He, the Spirit of truth, has come, He will guide you into all truth; for He will not speak on His own authority, but whatever He hears He will speak; and He will tell you things to come" (John 16:12–13).

Earlier we said that we need to confirm the things of God by His Word if we want to operate in His truth. Here it is, just one place among many in the Bible where Jesus confirms our ability to communicate with the Father, letting us know that the spirit of truth would come after He left.

Ok, now we have talked about God's still small voice, His use of other people, communication through circumstances, and communication through His Word. Now, I want to touch on God's loud voice, His corrective tone, the urgent attention getting aspect of communication with Him. Let me be very clear about this, I personally have never experienced God's external audible voice, at least I don't think so. However, three times I heard His voice so loud in my spirit, it seemed audible, let me explain. This loud voice I am talking about is distinctly different than the still small spiritual voice, which can be almost like a thought or a feeling. Consider the times God needed to discipline and/or correct specific individuals in the Bible.

"Then the Lord God called to Adam and said to him, "Where are you?" (Gen. 3:9).

This occasion when God "called" Adam, immediately after he made the choice to sin, reminds me of my need for discipline and correction early in my relationship with God. All three times I experienced this loud voice were early on in my spiritual walk, and it seemed remarkably like a human voice. However, I am reasonably sure it has been a spiritual voice every time; here is how I came to that conclusion. Twice, the voice spoke so loudly in my bedroom it awakened me, severely startling me both times. Both times after the incident I looked over and my wife was sound asleep. I couldn't believe she slept through that, but it could be because it was in the spirit. It is possible for those around to hear God's audible voice as He speaks. Saul and those around him on the road to Damascus are a good example of the external voice God sometimes uses. *"And the men who journeyed with him stood speechless, hearing a voice but seeing no one"* (Acts 9:7).

One of the things I mentioned as part of God's loud voice was His corrective tone, an attention getting corrective tone. This particular visit was about me slipping back into sin after committing to walk with God. I had asked my now wife, girlfriend then, to move back in with me after we had been walking with God and serving Him for a season. It seemed like a good, almost natural move to me, as she was losing her place of residence and had no place to go. It was one of those moves that I didn't really feel that guilty about, and until God convicted me this particular night, it felt almost normal. Looking back I believe that was due in part to my young Christian experience, also to the fact that we had lived together out of wedlock previously, and the fact that it is a widely accepted practice in the world these days.

Around 3:00 a.m. one morning, I was awakened to the sound of someone talking loudly in my bedroom. The noise startled me so badly, that by the time I realized it wasn't somebody in my room, I already had my nightstand drawer half open in thoughts of self-defense. The Lord spoke plain and clear, He said, "You can't grow anymore in me, you can't grow further as a teacher, until you fix this." But we basically talked it out, I remember asking God for guidance. "What do I do, Lord? Kick her out on the street?" We just had a conversation and came up with a solution together, it felt good to commit to God. We agreed that, for now, Steph and I would not sleep together, and if we hadn't gotten married by such and such date, I would end the relationship. You see, I had trust issues, among other things, after my past life of turmoil. God knows how to help us grow through our problems as we learn to trust Him. Now I felt like God was in this with me, wanting it to turn out right, but counting on me to stand up and follow through no matter which way it went.

Look what Jesus tells us about His personal relationship with the Father, *"For I have not spoken on my own authority; but the Father who sent me gave me a command, what I should say and what I should speak. And I know that His command is everlasting life. Therefore, whatever I speak, just as the Father has told me, so I speak"* (John 12:49-50).

Jesus Christ himself did not speak or do anything on His own authority, but just as the Father has told Him, that's what He said and did. So, if Jesus, savior of the world, trusted only in God and only did what He heard God say, then how much more should that hold true for us? How much more do we need to listen to His voice for guidance and direction? For me His voice and guidance are priceless, I tried life without seeking His guidance, and I never want to be in that place again!

Time went by and we did get married just as the conversation and agreement with God had outlined. At the time of this writing, Stephanie and I have been married and growing closer every day for over sixteen years. Hmm, seems like His guidance and instruction worked, just as it always does. With God first, Stephanie is my business partner, ministry partner, and life partner, we are as one flesh, together in Him. As the scripture says, *"Though one may be overpowered by another, two can withstand him. And a threefold cord is not quickly broken"* (Eccl. 4:12).

EIGHT

Following His Voice

As I said in previous chapters, hearing His voice is so important, but it brings with it a new set of challenges. Once we've gotten to the place where we have discerned who we listen to and we look forward to hearing His voice; now we risk disobedience if we do not follow that voice.

If I had not been able to communicate with God, I might have missed the greatest blessing in my life, someone compatible to share it with. I don't think I would have made the decision to get remarried without Him, and He knew it. He also knew I needed help to be able to do His work, to walk in my calling as a teacher and minister. My close communication with God keeps me on the right path. If I'm not doing His work, I don't stay as close, and when I don't stay close, I can begin to drift, and it becomes harder to hear His voice. If I'm not careful I can find myself beginning to see things from a worldly perspective.

My wife tends to keep me in check on staying close to God. She knows things do not flow as well when I'm not close to Him and regularly serving Him. As I have jokingly heard before, a spouse can be the second Holy Spirit when we need them to. Without her love, support, and confidence in me, things could be very different in our lives. She is one of the greatest blessings I thank God for every day. When you have a godly spouse, you have the ability to hold each other accountable when needed before things get too far away from God. And just like in our relationship with God, communication with our spouse is key. Scripture says, *"He who finds a wife finds what is good and receives favor from the Lord"* (Prov. 18:22) NIV.

The 3:00 a.m. conversation in my bedroom wasn't the last time God spoke to me loudly and urgently concerning our marriage. The second conversation was a little different, still with a sense of urgency, not corrective, but informative.

Let me back up a little, we had finally set a date for our wedding, and less than a week prior to that I was involved in an automobile accident on the highway at 70 mph. The air bags went off and I was transported by ambulance to the hospital, but I was released soon after being checked out.

Days later was our wedding on a Saturday at 5 o'clock in the evening. As I woke up that morning, I felt a little off, but I figured it was just nerves. It got worse throughout the day, and by the time of the wedding I was sweating and felt like I had a fever. We were supposed to leave for our honeymoon the next day, but when we got home, after the wedding, I was running a fever of 102.5°, along with teeth chattering chills, intense sheet soaking episodes of sweating, and painful body aches. We tried the normal medicines and treatments, but I kept getting worse throughout the night with my fever rising to 104° at one point. As I lay there around 3 a.m., God spoke up, very loudly. But this time He seemed excited, "You did it!" He spoke. It was a childlike excitement from God, the Creator of the universe. I could sense that He was well pleased with us because we were now married, and it felt good to know

He was with us. Then He added, "You are going to go into the hospital for a week and it's going to hurt." And He said "You will come out afterwards better off than when you went in." And then a female name came to me, Rebecca, I wasn't sure what that meant, but it felt like the conversation with God was over.

As I sat there contemplating what had just happened, my symptoms were getting worse, with ongoing cold chills, pain, and uncontrollable shaking. So I called the hospital I had been taken to after my automobile accident, which was about forty-five minutes away from our home. Rebecca answered the phone! An almost instant peace came over me as I was telling her my symptoms. The name Rebecca was the Lord's way of letting me know I was on the right track, with over a dozen hospitals within the same or less distance, I immediately knew this one was the right one.

After this conversation it was almost 4:00 a.m., but I was so excited, I had to wake up Stephanie and tell her, teeth chattering, shaking, and all. After my symptoms relaxed enough to ride in the car, she took me in to the hospital where I was admitted. After four days of test after test, numerous bouts of 104.5° fever, chills, pain, and shaking, my symptoms subsided. On the sixth day I was released, the diagnosis was "fever of unknown origin."

During that stay, even though I had no health insurance, and we weren't sure how we would pay, we had total peace. Our "honeymoon in the hospital" was a time of peace, prayer, and trust in God. We didn't know how we would come out better, but we knew it would happen because God said it would. And it did.

When the doctor came in, he mentioned that sometimes breathing in the dust and chemicals that deploy along with the air bag can cause medical issues. He went on to say that I should call my automobile insurance company and check on my personal injury protection. I was amazed, we received the full amount to cover all the hospital bills, plus another eleven thousand for pain and suffering. That was definitely coming out better than we went in, just as the Lord promised. We experienced the peace that surpasses all understanding, we trusted God together, and we were blessed financially, emotionally, and spiritually.

Direct communication with God became our source for everything good in our lives. From that point forward we began to see things really change in all areas of life. Hearing, following, and trusting in Him put us in a place where our faith could grow. It's a good thing too, because even though things were good, there were still plenty of challenges to deal with in our new life in Christ. The major difference now was the way we faced and dealt with those challenges, following His voice in obedience has been the key to our success. God will never intentionally lead you into the darkness of sin.

In the next chapter we will discuss how we handle conflict, troubles, challenges, and hardships. But first, let's talk more about where these difficulties come from in our newfound Christian walk.

Actually, sickness, disease, lack, death, and anything that's not of God comes from the same place it always has, the enemy. In First Peter, he tells us this:

"Be sober, be vigilant; because your adversary the devil walks about like a roaring lion, seeking whom he may devour" (1 Peter 5:7).

One of the biggest lies the enemy would have you believe is that God puts these troubles on us. That is simply not true as scripture tells us in many different places, and it is not God's design for us. What is true is the fact that we live in a sin filled world where sickness, disease, and evil exist. Why? We must back up all the way to the events that took place in the garden of Eden to get that answer, *"So He drove out the man; and He placed cherubim at the east of the Garden of Eden, and a flaming sword which turned every way, to guard the way to the tree of life"* (Gen. 3:24).

Because Adam and Eve sinned, they could no longer remain in the garden because sin cannot exist in God's domain. If sin and God do not co-exist, how would God put evil sin filled things upon us? He would not; because of Adam and Eve, we now dwell in a world where sin is all around us. Look what God told Cain before he killed his brother, Abel:

> *"If you do well, will you not be accepted? And if you do not do well, sin lies at the door. And its desire is for you, but you should rule over it"* (Gen. 4:7).

God warned Cain that sin desired him, therefore he had a choice to deny the anger he had against Abel, but he did not. In the very next verse, Cain acted on his anger instead of ruling over it as God told him to do, *"Now Cain talked with Abel his brother, and it came to pass, when they were in the field, that Cain rose up against Abel his brother and killed him"* (Gen. 4:8).

We rule over sin by not acting on our desire when we are tempted. The enemy has the ability to influence our thoughts if we let him, but the ultimate choice is ours. So the phrase "The devil made me do it" is not true, he cannot force us into anything. This is the most common form of spiritual warfare, resisting our own desire to sin. Jesus was tempted by the devil in the wilderness in the exact same manner, He is our example of how to resist. Look what James, the Lord's brother, says about the process of sin that has the ability to lead us into spiritual death.

> *"But each one is tempted when he is drawn away by his own desires and enticed. Then, when desire has conceived, it gives birth to*

sin; and sin, when it is full grown brings forth death" (James 1:14–15).

It's our choice; every time we are tempted, will we be drawn away from God? God and sin do not work together. If we walk toward our earthly, sin filled desires, then we are moving away from God. That's the enemy's plan in a nutshell, using the enticement of sin to pull us away from God and the church.

Once we are moving away from God instead of toward Him, it becomes harder and harder to hear His voice; then we hear the voices of the world, and of our own desires calling to us, enticing us, and that becomes a choice. If we choose to act on that sinful desire, it can begin to lead us down a dark path if we let it. Once we give in, it becomes easier to justify the same or similar sin the next time, and on and on it goes. We can easily see this in the natural world. It's the very reason law enforcement uses an M.O., or method of operation, to catch serial criminals.

Often, a repeat offender can find ways to become more efficient at their crimes. That's why there are things like the habitual criminal act, and the sex offender registry. The term hardened criminal applies to a person who will not stop his criminal activity, one who seems to completely lack self-control and remorse.

It's very much the same in the spiritual realm, ongoing sin can pull us away from God, and lead us into more sin. From there, we move farther and farther away from Him as our hearts slowly become hardened and our understanding is darkened. As individuals, we tend to stick to certain areas where we are most tempted, but it's not the first time the enemy has used temptation to lure someone into sin, *"No temptation has overtaken you except such as is common to man; but God is faithful, who will not allow you to be tempted beyond what you are able, but with the temptation will also make the way of escape, that you may be able to bear it"* (1 Cor. 10:13).

No sin is new, the enemy was not more clever as he attacked me, but I fell for the same old thing. The same temptations have been around for centuries, but one thing never changes, you always have a way out, a choice to make, a way of escape.

How do we stay out of sin to begin with by resisting temptation when it comes our way? The same way Jesus did. Jesus was prepared for the temptation because He was in constant communication with the Father. *"Then Jesus was led by the Spirit into the wilderness to be tempted by the devil."* (Matthew 4:1) We need to be prepared as well, expecting attacks and temptations as we pursue a godly life. Scripture warns us in many places, we need to take heed:

> *"Therefore rejoice, O heavens, and you who dwell in them! Woe to the inhabitants of the earth and the sea! For the devil has come down to you, having great wrath, because he knows that he has a short time"* (Rev. 12:12).

A big part of resisting temptation is being aware of what is coming, so we are not caught off guard. All these warnings in scripture about the enemy do us no good if we are not prepared to resist when turbulence comes. Remember how we said that the most common way God speaks to us is through His Word, the Bible? We have looked at several verses already where scripture warns us about the enemy. He is real and he comes to steal, kill, and destroy. I have heard it taught that the enemy knows our weaknesses and what temptation we are likely to give in to. Well, if he does, it's only because they are common to man, he is not all knowing. He only knows what works with mankind. He knows we are human, fallen, predictable, and we don't stand a chance without Jesus. But, good news, Jesus has made the way for us, think about the last part of the verse in John 10:

> *"I have come that they may have life, and that they may have it more abundantly"* (John 10:10).

Part of that abundant life is the defeat of the enemy on the cross, overcoming sin and death so we can have relationship with God, hearing, listening, and following His direction. As we have already seen, to follow God's voice we must first hear it, discerning the truth. In the next chapter we will look closely at how to deal with the noise and worldly confusion that tries to interfere with our godly communication. This is what is commonly known as spiritual warfare. Let's take a look at how we overcome the enemy in certain areas of our walk! One passage comes to mind as we prepare to move into chapter nine of this book:

> *For though we walk in the flesh, we do not war according to the flesh. For the weapons of our warfare are not carnal but mighty in God for pulling down strongholds, casting down arguments and every high thing that exalts itself against the knowledge of God, bringing every thought into captivity to the obedience of Christ.* (2 Corinthians 10:3–5)

That means we have a chance to do something about our thoughts, and our desires, before they lead us into temptation. Taking our thoughts captive means choosing what we allow to take root in our mind. If it's not of God, cast it out. This gets easier as we act on it. The more we act on casting out those impure thoughts, the closer we stay to God. The closer we are to Him, the easier it is to see the problems coming before we act on emotion.

For example, anger is one area I have to deal with on a fairly regular basis. If I don't, it can lead me into acting out of emotion, rather than using sound godly wisdom to diffuse the situation. If

I can see the opportunity to get mad coming, I am one step ahead when it happens. I'm able to take my thoughts into captivity ahead of time. For example, I drive daily for my work, often during rush hour traffic when most drivers are in a hurry to get where they are going. This is prime time to get into a road rage situation; but I already know that, so I try to stay aware of the possibility. If it's something you have fallen into in the past, there is a really good chance that you will have to deal with it again. So, when I see an aggressive driver, I begin to pray, asking God ahead of time to help me react as a man of God should. If the bird does flip, and the cuss words come at me, it's a lot easier to react in a manner that will diffuse the situation if I have already been praying about it. At that point, I have already pulled God's word into the situation, whether it be the still small voice within, or the word of God that dwells in me richly. Then I feel accountable for my immediate actions, able to resist and move on, usually waving and smiling, as I think about God being well pleased with me. This is overcoming the enemy!

And yes, there are times when we don't see it coming until it is right in our face. This is when being "prayed up" comes into play. A close relationship with God keeps us thinking of Him, and all He has done for us. It's a lot easier to react in a godly manner when we are already in His presence through prayer, worship, and/or communication. What is already in our hearts and minds is what is most likely to rise up when the opportunity to fall back into sin presents itself.

Recently, I had a sudden conflict at a crowded gas station that arose before I could see it coming. There were about twenty-five pumps, all of them full, so I started praying for one to open up, suddenly someone pulled away from one near me, so I pulled in. As I was already outside of the truck putting my card into the pump to get it started, I noticed a car, backing up fast and headed right for my vehicle. I thought, "This guy doesn't see me, he is going to back right into my truck!" I reached in through my open window and tapped the horn. The car stopped inches from my front bumper and a young man, mid- to late-twenties, gets out and starts angrily yelling at me, saying that I took his gas pump. He cursed and screamed at me, then he asked; didn't you see me headed for that pump? I said "No, actually, I did not," but he didn't hear it, he was too busy yelling. My first thoughts as this muscular, physically fit young man came toward me were thoughts from my previous life, the way I would have defended myself before my walk with God. Thoughts of carnal warfare tried to enter into my thought process. I grabbed the gas handle and thought of soaking him down if he came close enough. Immediately, I consciously knew that thought was not of God, I knew because I had already been in communication with Him before I ever pulled into the station. I then started looking at the brick pillar beside me, I thought, slamming his head into this will slow him down, but I knew that wasn't right either. God checked me in my spirit. Keep in mind, all of this happened in seconds, it was almost like slow motion as I was able to think through all these things. God stopped me in my actions as I was now about to pull my knife out of my right front pocket. I said in my thoughts, Lord, what would you have me do, let him kill me? I suddenly heard the words of Jesus:

"Blessed are the peacemakers, for they shall be called sons of God" (Matthew 5:9).

Right then I had a thought, I reached into my truck through the open window again, acting like I was reaching for a weapon. This immediately stopped the man in his tracks, about two feet away from me. I tried to stay in peace as he got back in his car and drove off, but my thoughts began to stray. Pride tried to enter in, the wrong voice began to speak, "You let him get away with cussing you out!" Before I let it go any further, I called a pastor friend, and within minutes we were beyond that conversation and talking ministry.

Sometimes, we need help to keep from listening to the wrong voice and seeking godly council is often a good option. God has placed people in your path, brothers and sisters who face the same things you do. So, maybe it wasn't easy, but God's voice along with a trusted mentor to speak with helped me stay away from acting contrary to godly wisdom.

As I said, I was communicating with God and praying before I pulled into that gas station. I was not prepared for the confrontation because I saw it coming, but because I was in a good place of fellowship with God. Being at peace in the beginning helped me to slow down and to listen, instead of flying off the handle and becoming just like the man who was in my face. If I had been listening to heavy metal rock music, as I often did in my life before God, the outcome could have been much different. Communication with God is key to being able to work through an otherwise volatile situation, while taking worldly thoughts into captivity. This man was well beyond listening to reason, but because I was in a place where I could hear the Lord's voice, God made a way out. Hearing and following His voice are imperative to overcoming the enemy, as we will see more of in the next chapter.

NINE

Overcoming the Enemy

First, I would like to discuss the title choice I made for this chapter. I chose "Overcoming" the enemy rather than "Defeating" the enemy for a specific reason; Jesus has already defeated Satan for us.

"I am he who lives, and was dead, and behold, I am alive forevermore. Amen. And I have the keys of Hades and of Death" (Rev. 1:18).

Jesus has defeated hell, death, and the grave through the cross; it's already done. But that doesn't mean the enemy can't attempt to torment us in our thoughts. The devil knows, just as we do, that Jesus is coming back, so he is doing all he can to wreak havoc as much as he can, for as long as he can. Let's look again at Jesus's words in the gospel of John:

> *"The thief does not come except to steal, and to kill, and to destroy. But I have come that they may have life , and that they may have it more abundantly"* (John 10:10).

Jesus has made the way for us to be victorious over the enemy, but we still have a major part to play, the ultimate choice is ours. As I said way back in the preface of this book, the spiritual realm is not black-and-white, it takes faith to operate in the promises contained in scripture. We already saw what Hebrews 11 says about it, but it's worth taking a closer look in the context of this chapter:

> *"But without faith it is impossible to please Him, for he who comes to God must believe that He is, and that He is a rewarder of those who diligently seek Him"* (Heb. 11:6).

Let's talk about this specific scripture, what does the author of Hebrews mean here? Look at what is said, and what is not said, in this particular verse. Let's consider what is not said so we can focus on the true meaning. He does not say without faith we cannot receive salvation, nor does he say our sins can't be forgiven without faith, even though both statements are definitely true. The writer is going beyond the basic benefits of our salvation; he is talking about maximizing our potential to do God's work in this life, and about receiving in the next life according to those works we do now. So, let's back that up with scripture to ensure we have the correct understanding of this important verse. First, let's confirm that we have rewards in this life when we diligently seek to serve Him. Look at the words of Paul:

> *For if I preach the gospel, I have nothing to boast of, for necessity is laid upon me; yes, woe is me if I do not preach the gospel! For if I do this willingly, I have a reward; but if against my will, I have been entrusted with a stewardship. What is my reward then? That when I preach the gospel, I may present the gospel of Christ without charge, that I may not abuse my authority in the gospel* (1 Corinthians 9:16–18).

Paul is talking about preaching the gospel, doing God's work in this life. Let's focus on the specific rewards he is speaking of in the last verse of our passage. *"What is my reward then?"* The reward is God helping him to preach the gospel according to His plan, which is also *our* reward in this life, our gifts! I can think of no greater reward in this life than my heavenly Father guiding me into ministry, to His glory, as I do His work. The spiritual reward in this life is being able to honor God with our gifts; for me that is teaching and preaching in the power of Christ.

Now, let's look at the rewards that we are building up for the next life, knowing that using the rewards we have in this life helps us build rewards for the next. Jesus speaks specifically about this, as recorded by the apostle John in the Book of Revelation:

> *And behold, I am coming quickly, and my reward is with Me, to give to everyone according to his work. I am the Alpha and the Omega, the Beginning and the End, the First and the Last. **Blessed are those who do His commandments, that they may have the***

right to the tree of life, and may enter through the gates into the city (Revelation 22:12–14).

Did you catch that? We looked at Genesis 3:24 back in chapter eight? We saw that God had driven the man out of the garden of Eden, placed cherubim east of the garden, and set a flaming sword to guard the way to the tree of life. Now, in the Book of Revelation, Jesus tells us that those who do His commandments will have the right to the tree of life! What Adam and Eve lost through sin; Jesus restores through the cross. This is part of what I meant by Jesus going full circle for us. This is the power of the cross mentioned in 1 Corinthians 1:18, which we read earlier in this book. Jesus already took back everything the enemy tried to steal and made His power available to us so we can overcome enemy attacks in His strength, in *this* life. Now, in Revelation, Jesus mentions specific rewards available to us when He comes back, rewards according to our works for the *next* life!

The enemy would like nothing more than to discourage us, deceive us, and steal our rewards from us, but he is extremely limited in power; he can't force us to do anything. His power lies in the ability to influence our choices, to tempt us through worldly situations, to bring division into Christ's body, and ultimately to cause us to turn from God. We must stand strong in the power of Christ by adhering to godly principles and staying close to our Father.

In the chapters leading up to this one, we have covered many scriptural techniques and teachings that all lead us to this chapter on overcoming the enemy. Let's review some of these as we move toward better understanding spiritual warfare.

In chapter 1 we looked at the differences between a Kingdom Perspective and a worldly perspective. Seeing things as God sees them is truth; knowledge of the truth keeps us from falling for the lies of the enemy.

Chapter 2 was about the power of our testimony, acknowledging what God has already brought us through as we face new battles and temptations.

The design for chapter 3 was to show us the power of our choices. Every choice we make has the ability to lead us closer to God or to pull us away from Him.

The power of forgiveness, grace, and mercy is prevalent throughout chapter 4, leading us into a personal relationship with our heavenly Father.

Chapter 5 begins to show us the stability that comes from truly knowing our Lord and Savior and how a relationship with Him helps keep us on the right path.

These first five chapters help us build a solid foundation on which to stand as we navigate life. This solid foundation *is* our relationship with God, which allows us to hear His voice and receive knowledge, guidance, and wisdom directly from our Father. Jesus shows us this by asking His disciples a question that none of them could answer correctly except Peter, *"He said to them, But who do you say that I am? Simon Peter answered and said, you are the Christ, the son of the living God. Jesus answered and said to him, Blessed are you Simon Bar-Jonah, for flesh and blood has not revealed this to you, but My Father who is in heaven"* (Matthew 16:15–17).

This is further scriptural proof that we can "hear" from God and receive knowledge that does not come from man. Furthermore, it only happens through a relationship with Jesus Christ. But it's in the next verse where Jesus reveals a key point, *"And I also say to you that you are Peter, and on this rock I will build My church, and the gates of Hades shall not prevail against it"* (Matthew 16:16–18).

Jesus built His church on the solid foundation of being able to receive wisdom directly from the Father! This is how we overcome the enemy; revelation knowledge can show us the truth when we are in the midst of battle. Knowing God and having a personal relationship with Him are the foundation, the rock, our walk is based on. Once we have that solid footing underneath us, we can truly begin to grow in faith as we grow in Him.

Chapters six, seven, and eight show us benefits of our relationship with God that can carry us through our battles all the way to victory.

Chapter 6 shows us how to use the Word in our lives and how to have Jesus working alongside us in everything we do. We must have the faith to believe, not only what we read, but what we receive directly from Him.

In chapter 7 we said that hearing from God often does not require the use of our physical ears. We can learn to "listen" in many other ways.

As we moved into chapter 8 we began to see the importance of doing what we hear Him say, not wanting to miss the blessings and fruits that come from a relationship with Him. Obedience to our Heavenly Father brings stability into our lives.

Which leads us right here, into the middle of chapter nine, where we are putting all the tools from the preceding chapters into overcoming enemy attacks. Let me use testimony from life experience to show the Lord's power as He leads, guides, and directs a healing situation. To confirm power of testimony from the Word of God, let's remind ourselves of a previously mentioned passage we discussed in chapter two, *"And they overcame Him by the blood of the Lamb and by the word of their testimony, and they did not love their lives to the death"* (Rev. 12:11).

The testimony I will use here is a personal testimony of healing that my wife and I experienced a number of years ago. There are so many things to see in this example, I will try not to miss any points and at the same time focus primarily on the keys. The purpose of testimony in this book is to see God's Word coming to life, seeing the actual principles moving off of the pages and into our everyday lives. I want you to keep something in mind as we discuss this particular occasion; God doesn't always operate the way *we* think He should. Yes, of course, He can heal supernaturally, instantly, and miraculously, but that is not always the way He chooses. The Lord has all things to consider, and remember, He is *"not willing that any should perish but that all should come to repentance"* (2 Peter 3:9).

At the time of this testimony I was at a particular church doing the work of an Associate Pastor, Teacher, and Elder for a season. It was on Christmas Eve around midafternoon when I was taking a shower, getting ready to go to our family event that night. While in the shower, I felt a golf ball sized lump in my upper right thigh that I had never noticed before. Stephanie and I prayed and felt like we should go to the doctor, this could be serious, and we know the Lord sometimes uses doctors and medicine to do His work.

Being Christmas Eve, we went to one of the few places that was open, a minor emergency clinic near our home. The on-duty doctor looked at the lump and immediately sent us to the ER in a larger town thinking I had a blood clot. He was genuinely concerned and told us to go now, immediately, and do not stop. My wife drove us and she prayed the entire forty minute ride to the hospital, right then I felt a peace come over me as she prayed. That peace would guard and keep my thoughts from running wild during the entire six-week ordeal to come.

We got to the ER and the doctor immediately sent me for scans, and afterward, she discussed the findings with us. She told us they saw and measured the lump on the scan. They were still thinking it was a blood clot but were not sure what caused it. She sent us home and told us to keep an eye on it, "If anything changes, get back to an ER immediately," she said in a serious tone.

The next day, Christmas Day, a little over twenty-four hours later, the mass had already gotten noticeably bigger, so we went back to the same hospital. A different ER doctor saw us and told us it was not a blood clot, much to our surprise. He said, "I am not sure what it is, but it's not a clot, let's do some different scans today."

As the results came back, he told us it was not a blood clot, it was a mass, a tumor, and he recommended a surgeon, saying it would have to come out. He went on to say, "We can't tell if it's cancer for sure, without doing a biopsy, and there is no point in doing a biopsy because it has to come out. But, with your age, (late 40s at that time), and as fast as it is growing, it must be cancer. But you will be ok with chemo and radiation after the surgery. I had peace, knowing that God had me no matter what came of this situation.

We went home and prayed, and the Lord spoke to me in my spirit, clearly saying, "It is not cancer, and you will not have chemotherapy or radiation or anything like it."

I had to get an appointment with my primary care doctor, to get a referral for insurance purposes. My personal family doctor told me there was a good chance it was not cancer, and it turned out that he would be the only doctor to encourage me in that manner throughout the entire process. It felt good to have at least one doctor who lined up with what God had spoken to me!

It was more than two weeks since the initial clinic visit before we could get in to see the surgeon for a consultation. By this time the mass had grown tremendously, so much you could see it even with my jeans on. The surgeon did a new scan and showed us where the mass had fingers, or tentacles, that were growing down into my muscle. He said that he would not touch this because it was too involved for him, and he recommended another surgeon. Long story short, two more surgeons told us the same thing, and all of them said it was cancer without ever doing a biopsy.

Finally, we found a "world-renowned surgical oncologist" who said he would do it. (The world-renowned part came from a magazine cover hanging in his waiting room.) He seemed excited as he showed us the scan and how he was going to have to cut into the muscle to remove the tumor. He also mentioned the fact that it had to be cancer, and they would biopsy it once it was taken out. Furthermore, the biopsy would determine if we had to do chemotherapy, or radiation, or both. That statement did not faze me, I knew better so I stayed in faith, hanging on to the words the Lord had spoken to me. The surgeon said it would be a four-hour surgery, I would be in the hospital for two or three days and recovery time would be six to eight weeks, with the possibility of rehabilitation therapy being necessary, because of the muscle being cut.

As he continued to speak, something *did* faze me, it was a statue on his desk, a see-through, acrylic, tubular cylinder standing upright on a base. Inside of the cylinder I could see gold metal stars and ribbons and the word "God" written in gold letters curving around inside the cylinder. This was the strangest Christian symbol I had ever seen; or was it? I interrupted him in mid-sentence, asking, "are you a Christian?" I will never forget his response, "No, but I am a god-fearing man" he said. I wasn't sure what that meant, so I rephrased the question, "do you believe in Jesus Christ?" He said No and went back to talking about the surgery in detail. At that point I could hear nothing he said from then on. His response rattled me, and I was concerned.

My wife and I left his office and were walking down a quiet hallway of the medical building. I was discouraged telling her how we would have to find another surgeon, since this one was not a Christian. That's when God spoke to me, strongly, saying, "You're not in *his* hands, you're in My hands, and this is right where I want you!"

That was all He said, but it was enough to restore my peace just as fast as it had left me. So we went ahead and scheduled the surgery, it was early February before we could get it done, almost six weeks after we found the lump. By this point it had grown so much I could no longer wear jeans, only loose-fitting sweats or stretch pants.

The morning of the surgery something had happened, it's like it had almost doubled in size overnight! It was now a protrusion hanging off of the side of my leg, it was huge! My wife and I were glad it was being removed that day, and we proceeded to the hospital.

I woke up after the surgery to find my wife smiling big, as she stood at the foot of my hospital bed. She told me that it went really well, and the doctors seemed incredibly pleased with the results. About that time, the surgeon's primary assistant walked into the room, also with a big smile on his face. "It went well," he said, and then he told me he could not explain what had happened. He said, "It's as if something encapsulated the tumor, and we just removed it. It was not intertwined with the muscle as the scans had shown, so it was not necessary to cut into the muscle as expected. Yet he still had to tell me that it was cancer, and the biopsy would determine the treatment! With that said, I couldn't help but give

God glory, I told him it wasn't something, but someone, who had encapsulated the tumor and that's why he could not explain it. He looked at me, surprised, as he walked out of the room, but I didn't care, I was just ready for God to let them know what we already knew! The truth would be revealed soon.

The surgery took about two hours instead of the expected four, and no muscle cutting was necessary. It went so well that he sent me home about an hour later, so I was home that evening, not after two or three days in the hospital as expected. I was back working in two days, not weeks. As I'm sure you have perceived by now, the biopsy came back clear, no cancer, just like God said, contrary to what many of the doctors had spoken. As the scripture says, *"Now to him who is able to do exceedingly abundantly above all that we ask or think , according to the power that works in us"* (Eph. 3:20).

Now, let's look at the biblical truth in this personal testimony, I want us to further see how God's word weaves into our everyday lives, and how the power of faith in God's word, the spirit of truth, can change things in our natural physical lives. Faith is key, and I want us to see how

God was right there with me through the entire ordeal, keeping me strong in faith, leaving no room for doubt.

God never left me during this process of healing. He spoke to me several times when I needed to know He was there; when the negativity came, His voice prevailed. He gave me the choice to focus on His voice, rather than the negativity that was all around. In fact, He prepared me, telling me up front that it was not cancer, no chemo or radiation would be required. When five out of six doctors spoke cancer, I didn't buy it! I was able to hold to what God said instead, what His voice told me. This kept me on track and in faith so I could remain in His plan and purpose without doubting.

I have to say something here, because of things I have seen other Christians do in similar circumstances. I did not deny that the tumor was there, nor did I argue with each doctor who said it was cancer. I just held to God's word in faith as they spoke, letting it play out to the end. The final word came when the biopsy came back clear, no cancer, which was the truth of the situation. All the rest was just speculation. Each doctor saying it was cancer was just voicing his opinion, based on education and past experience. Look what Paul says about that:

> *"For the wisdom of this world is foolishness with God"* (1 Cor. 3:19).

These doctors were speaking from a worldly perspective, years of medical practice, and decades of education to get where they were. This particular surgical oncologist had worked his way up to becoming one of the absolute best, most respected surgeons in his field in the world. From a worldly perspective we must respect that authority and allow God to work. I was only seeing things from a Kingdom Perspective because of the grace of God, *not* because I was smarter than them. This is a good example of a time when we need to get out of the way and let God work. It's our job to plant seeds, stay in faith, and follow God's promptings; it's not our job to argue, debate, or force people into believing the same way we do.

I actually saw a woman get up in a doctor's face and argue when he walked in with x-ray results, saying her husband's wrist was broken. She said,

"We don't accept that!" She was basically calling the doctor a liar, instead of trusting God to heal. All this did was bring stress and strife into an otherwise peaceful situation. We cannot deny the truth, but we can trust God to heal over and above the expected results.

Another good example, was when I walked into a Bible study and said, "My wife can use your prayers, she is sick today." I was blasted, cursed, and rebuked by everyone in that class for saying she was sick. I reminded them that Jesus uses the word sick over ten times in the gospels, all in the context of healing. Would we really rebuke Jesus to His face if He were standing in front of us, telling us to go heal the sick, as He did many times in the Bible? Of course not, and we shouldn't be so quick to rebuke other people either. Jesus Himself said the well are not in need of a physician, but the sick, if someone is not sick, then why do we need to pray for physical healing.

We need to work with God when it comes to healing, not against the doctors, and not against people He has sent to care for us. If you saw a man with an amputation, would you really walk up to him and say, "That leg is not missing?" Can you see that it's the same principle when we rebuke someone for speaking the physical truth that is right in front of our eyes? Healing has been mistaught in this area. We will stick to scripture, stick to how Jesus operated and not how man operates. Rebuke the sickness and it's right to be there as we cast it out in Jesus's name, but we can't deny the fact that it is there.

Next, let's look at how God chose to heal, according to our testimony in His plan and not mine. Obviously, our natural mind wants to take the easy way out, but that's not always God's plan for us. If He had just healed me instantaneously, supernaturally removed the tumor, a lot of things would have been different. For one, my faith would not have grown as it did along the way, throughout the process. And my faith growing was just fruit, a side benefit that comes from serving God, a building block to strengthen me in Him. Remember when I said we are in partnership with God, doing His work? Sometimes we need to endure hard things for the sake of that partnership, so His glory can be revealed through us.

The doctors involved would not have been exposed to the truth, the fact that this was not cancer, even though everything in them said it was. All their training, education, and experience was challenged when they misdiagnosed cancer and experienced things they could not explain.

Another thing that would have been missed is something that I have not told you yet. While this process was happening, the Lord led me to start teaching a new series on healing in my Sunday morning Bible class. I questioned it, wondering why anyone would come to a class on healing when the teacher had a giant tumor growing in his leg? I had to wear loose pants and the lump could obviously be seen, furthermore, I couldn't stand and teach as I always had, so I sat on a stool instead.

I followed God's leading and began to announce the class to our church body. The first day, our normally ten-to-fifteen-person class had forty people show up, on time, in their seats, ready to go! I did not see that coming, but God did, He set it up for His body, the body of Christ. People stood with me and wanted to support me, as well as see God at work. They prayed and stood on the word God had given me, that the tumor was not cancer. When it was out, the tumor measured nine inches long, by six inches wide, by one and a half inches thick and was not cancerous. When our class found out the final outcome, the applause, hallelujahs, and praise to God rattled that room for minutes, giving Him all glory! This was priceless, it touched my heart as I saw what God had done, among our church body, through me.

From this testimony you can see how the power of the Word, the ability to hear and listen to His voice, and the willingness to follow, all led to victory in this situation. Knowing that God was with us kept Steph and I at peace and able to hear and focus on His voice, all to His glory!

The result of all of this is not only to glorify God, but to help you and I prepare for the next enemy attack. That's how we overcome, by building up our trust in Him, knowing He has our back every time! Remember, we can't achieve victory unless there is something to overcome, that's when we bring in the power of testimony!

TEN

Walking in Victory

My grace is sufficient for you, for my strength is made perfect in weakness (2 Corinthians 12:9).

These were the Lord's words to Paul. God's grace is absolutely imperative to be able to walk in victory while serving Him. For Steph and I, our walk with God changed failure into success as we learned to listen, to hear His voice, and to trust Him in everything. Only grace allows this communication with our heavenly Father since we have all sinned and fallen short of the glory of God. Darkness has been replaced with light and hope for the future overcame the darkness we once knew. This transformation was easy to see for us, and for those around us as we grew up in Him.

Early in our walk with the Lord things changed drastically, many of them became directly opposite of what they once were. For example, before God I worked a job that was taking me nowhere, no benefits, no retirement, nothing to look forward to but hard work. I wanted to be self-employed, so I tried to start several different small businesses before walking with God, all to no avail. In fact, about a year before committing my life to God I thought I would try my hand in the vending business. I had three vending machines which I had purchased and put on locations, but the outcome didn't look good. As our lives began to change, so did the way we approached business. My wife and I began to pray and ask God for direction in our business, and He answered. Little by little, one step at a time, He began to lead us with specific instruction when we would ask. When needed, He would give us confirmation, prompting, or whatever it took to move us down His business path for us. We worked at our business part-time for a few years, and then went full-time in 2010. The three vending machines we started with grew to 135 machines at one point, and as of this writing I have sold down to about 80 machines in order to free up more time for ministry, including writing this book.

On my own, I tried several different businesses that failed because I was looking at it all wrong. I saw business from a worldly perspective as I was living life as the world lives at that time, I was focused on money, and how to make it, and I had none! As long as God was not much a part of my life or my business, nothing worked for me. Look what the book of James says about it:

> *Come now, you who say, "Today or tomorrow we will go to such and such a city, spend a year there, buy and sell, and make a profit;" whereas you do not know what will happen tomorrow. For what is your life? It is even a vapor that appears for a little time and then vanishes away. Instead you ought to say, "If the Lord wills, we shall live and do this or that. But now you boast in your arrogance. All such boasting is evil"* (James 4:13–16).

From a Kingdom Perspective we can see the problem with this situation, but more importantly we can see the solution. Instead of leaving God out of our plans, we need to give Him the biggest part in making them. A worldly perspective says we will start this business, do it this way, and do whatever it takes to make it work. Then we have the nerve to say, "Please bless our business, Lord." To walk in God's best for us we need to follow *His* direction for our business from the beginning. Asking Him to "bless our mess" after we have created it, takes God out of the decision-making process. At that point we are trying to figure out how to recover and rebuild instead of how to create it on a solid foundation. It took a total change in perspective before I could really prosper at business.

To put it simply, success in business came as we put God in charge and stayed out of the way. Instead of focusing primarily on income, we began to focus on hearing His voice and doing our best to follow spiritual promptings. Finally, I realized that the main purpose of our business is not to support my wife and I, that's just fruit. The main purpose of our business must be about the

Father's business, and then everything else falls into place. As Paul wrote, *"While we do not look at the things which are seen, but at the things which are not seen, for the things which are seen are temporary, but the things which are not seen are eternal"* (2 Cor. 4:18). This scripture describes the main difference between a worldly perspective and a Kingdom Perspective, it's all in what we choose to see.

A worldly perspective will only see things in this life, while a Kingdom Perspective sees this life as temporary, leading us into the next life and eternity with Him. From a Kingdom Perspective, I could see the truth, business is a ministry tool. At this time I have machines at about 40 different business locations, with 20–120 people at each location, and always changing. That's a lot of people to interact with, a lot of people watching my example, both directly and indirectly. So what is my most important job when it comes to ministry in business? Is it keeping my machines clean and in good working order because I represent the kingdom as God's child? Is it saying "God Bless," so people know I'm a Christian? Is it giving back to others because of a successful business? Is it putting scripture verses visibly on my machines to help spread God's Word? Is it giving my slow selling products to a food ministry to help the homeless?

Actually all of these can be effective, but the most important is just to be the man of God I've been called to be in His strength. But, as I have found out on many occasions, God's ways are not our ways. Sometimes, we may even be acting on something the Bible says, but we haven't sought *His* will for dealing with a certain situation.

For example, I have a vending machine in a blue-collar setting that is owned by a large company with many other locations. At this particular time, years ago, I had machines in two of their offices that I serviced on a regular basis. In one of these, I began to notice money missing, so I counted and documented for several weeks before taking any action. I counted $18.00 missing one week, $22.50 the next, and on and on for the next five or six weeks. Besides the money, it takes a lot more time to run a stop, because you have to inventory product every time you service a location; not to mention changing out locks in case someone has a key and taking other security measures. Finally, I proved to myself that I was being stolen from every week, and none of the security measures intended to stop it were working.

As I left the location one day, I was getting angry thinking about it, and I made up my mind that I would pull my machine out to stop the problem. As I was driving to my next location, I called "Dusty," who was the regional manager over both of the locations I had with his company. I told him the amounts of the losses each week, and the security measures I had taken to no avail. I said, "Dusty, at this point I have no choice but to pull the machine out of that location. I will pick it up soon, just wanted you to know as a courtesy, since we have always worked well together." He asked me if I would give him a chance to talk to his guys first, I said respectfully, "no, it's gone on long enough as it is, but thank you for allowing me to serve You as long as you did."

After we hung up the phone, I pulled into my next business location to service the machine I had there. As I was walking in, God spoke to me, in my spirit, loud but gently, as He began to ask questions. "How much money have you lost at that location?" Feeling righteous I answered, "Lord I know I have to be a good steward of the business you have given me, that's why I am pulling their machine." He responded, "That is not what I asked you, how much have you lost? I answered, "maybe $150.00 altogether Lord." The next words He spoke, affected me, as He sometimes speaks to us in the same manner as we speak to other people. "Is one soul for My Kingdom not worth that much to you?" He asked. I dropped to my knees right there in the parking lot as I confessed, repented, and said, "Of course it is, Lord; what do you want me to do?"

If I had only asked, "What do you want me to do?" before making my decision it would have saved me some trouble. But I'm sure the lesson in humility did me some good anyway. I called Dusty back, apologized for making a rash decision, and told him I would love to give him the chance to talk to his guys if he was still willing. He did, and I never lost another quarter at that location. In fact, over the next few years the company grew, and I was asked to install machines in four more of the company's locations, for a total of six. I cannot tell you exactly how much those additional locations brought in over the next few years, but it was in the neighborhood of several thousand dollars. That's not only victory, that's doing *"exceedingly abundantly above all that we ask or think, according to the power that works in us"* (Eph. 3:20).

As you can see, I am definitely not perfect at hearing and following His voice, but His grace is sufficient for me. A couple of weeks later, after the theft incident, the plant manager at that location, "Jose," caught me one rainy day after everyone else had left. He asked me why I would leave my machine at the location after being stolen from. This time I prayed before answering; remember how I said we must discern what to say and what not to say in a given situation? We will see the importance of that right here.

At God's prompting, I told Jose that I felt like it was what God wanted me to do. He began to tell me how he was raised going to a large Catholic church in Mexico City, but he didn't really believe in Jesus. Long story short, about forty-five minutes later, he gave his life to Jesus right there in the office. Look at the spiritual and financial blessings I would have missed if I'd not been able to hear the Lord's guidance, direction, and wisdom.

We are human, we make mistakes, but God does not. As long as we choose the righteous path, we can stay close to Him; when we are close to Him, we can hear His voice loud and clear. As long as we listen, He can lead us into, or out of, anything we face in this world. But we must choose our walk daily. Look at this poem which I wrote for The Teaching Room in 2019:

One Man's Walk

The path has been laid before him, the choice is in his hand,

He can choose to live for himself, or will he choose God's plan?

The walk isn't always easy, no matter what he decides,

But life with God beside him, will always change the tides.

No longer is he led away, by his own desires and enticed,

Life has purpose and meaning now, it's not just
a roll of the dice.

For each word he is responsible, and every
thought will count,

But the rules are not a burden, as the challenge
begins to mount.

With Jesus as his savior, and also as his Lord,

The word of God beside him, is sharper than
any sword.

The troubles are not absent, but still as real
as before,

The results for him are clear, God's love has
opened the door.

He now seeks first the kingdom, not after
fortune or fame,

For eternity he will know peace, in the book of
life, is his name!

In the love of Christ,
—Brother Gregg

Doing business and living life according to godly principles tends to get people's attention, because we operate differently than the world operates. It got Jose's attention so much that he started asking questions, and that's all God needed to work in that situation. Besides, running a business has plenty of challenges, so why face them alone? Think about that for a minute, every aspect of our business and our life can be used for ministry with God as our partner. So, what is His main goal?

> *"The Lord is not slack concerning His promise, as some count slackness, but is longsuffering toward us, not willing that any should perish but that all should come to repentance"* (2 Peter 3:9).

God wants to reach as many people as possible, so we need to look at our business relations with Him as a partnership. With any business partnership it must be profitable for both parties to be successful. To reach people He needs us, to thrive in this sin filled world, we need Him. Some people will choke on this, thinking I'm saying we're equal with God. That's not what I'm saying at all, but we should be working together with Him to reach a common goal. Our common goal is building His kingdom, and we must be willing to do whatever it takes to reach the lost and help build up His body, the body of Christ. Just like any business, the Father's business takes sacrifice and commitment to be successful. At the same time, our Father knows we have needs in this physical world and He leads us in a manner that helps fulfill those needs as we are doing His work. Let's remind ourselves what Matthew's gospel says about it, as we have already read these verses back in chapter one:

> *Therefore do not worry, saying, "What shall we eat?" or "What shall we drink?" or "What shall we wear?" For after all these things the Gentiles seek. For your heavenly Father knows that you need all these things. But seek first the kingdom of God and His righteousness, and all these things shall be added to you. Therefore do not worry about tomorrow, for tomorrow will worry about its own things. Sufficient for the day is its own trouble* (Matthew 6:31–34).

These few verses say more than I could say in a whole chapter. Seek God instead of wealth and your physical needs will be met as a part of serving Him. That doesn't mean it will be easy; it doesn't mean you won't have to work. It does mean you don't have to worry and stress over your basic needs, because God has your back.

As you can see, our business experiences definitely turned around when we put God first. Let's look at another aspect of our lives that changed drastically as we partnered with Him. This one is even more directly related to ministry and to my calling as a teacher of the Word of God.

Before God, you could probably say that I was an introvert, or at the least, very quiet. I remember my fear of speaking in groups, even small groups of family and friends. More than two people would start making me nervous and uneasy, and it became hard to concentrate on what I was saying. As I lived life without God, my sin kept me in fear in so many ways, this is just one example. I was afraid to speak because of fear that I would say something wrong. I was afraid people would find out how I really was on the inside. It was like I had a fear of people finding out I lived in fear. It caused me to be angry and unable to trust, thinking that most people were out to get me.

After I committed my life to God, my fear of speaking to groups was one of the first things to change, and it happened drastically and quickly. It began in small group settings, and before I knew it I was speaking to groups of fifty, seventy-five, and even more than a hundred people at times. Now, I tell people to be careful, you put me in front of a group talking about God and you may not be able to stop me. To His glory alone, I am now able to teach and preach the Word fearlessly and boldly in any setting. It's now a great privilege for me to get God's Word out clearly and accurately so people can understand and relate to it. God often turns our weaknesses into strong points for His glory, that those who knew us before cannot deny His power.

As I prepare to close this book, I want to challenge and encourage you to put the life lessons and experiences we've shared together throughout these pages to work in your life. Draw near to Him through daily communication, while doing your best to follow His promptings. Put God first, let Him lead, and get yourself out of the way when you need to. Trust His guidance to get you where you need to be as His child, serving Him in all you do. When you do run into challenges, confrontation, and hardship, make sure you face them from a Kingdom Perspective.

> *"Beloved, I pray that you may prosper in all things and be in health, just as your soul prospers"* (3 John 2).

John's prayer is my prayer for you as we both move deeper into our walk with God. Thank you so much for reading! My hope is that this book will help you grow closer to the Lord and be a blessing of encouragement to you and all those you encounter in ministry! I will leave you in the love of Christ with a poem I wrote through the prompting of the Holy Spirit in 2019.

Hope in Jesus

A life lived for Jesus is one that fulfills,

it consumes with a purpose and leads
where He wills.

Seek first the Kingdom and His mighty name,

The results are much better than wealth,
power, and fame.

With eternal rewards, and peace in this life,

His spirit puts an end to stress, worry, and strife.

Live not as the world, but as God says to do,

And those sleepless nights will surely leave you.

So let's thank the Lord for mercy and grace,

Faith, hope, and love to finish the race.

Thank you now Father for all that you've done.

We have hope of eternity, with you
and your son!

May God bless and keep you always!

—Brother Gregg